The Practice of School Reform

The Practice of School Reform

Lessons from Two Centuries

JAMES NEHRING

Foreword by
LARRY CUBAN

Published by
State University of New York Press, Albany

For information, contact State University of New York Press, Albany, NY
www.sunypress.edu

Production by Diane Ganeles
Marketing by Fran Keneston

Library of Congress Cataloging-in-Publication Data

Nehring, James.
  The practice of school reform : lessons from two centuries / James Nehring ; foreword
by Larry Cuban.
       p. cm.
  Includes bibliographical references and index.
  ISBN 978-1-4384-2845-1 (hardcover : alk. paper)
  ISBN 978-1-4384-2846-8 (pbk. : alk. paper)
  1. Public schools—United States—History. 2. Educational change—United
States—History. I. Title.

LA212.N44 2009
371.010973—dc22   2009003140

10 9 8 7 6 5 4 3 2 1

For my father,
who inspires confidence.

You are not obligated to complete the work, but neither are you free to abandon it.

—Rabbi Tarfon, *The Talmud*

You must be the change you wish to see in the world.

—attributed to Mohandas Gandhi

Contents

Foreword

James Nehring pulls no punches and hides no assumptions in this book. He is a thoughtful, passionate, progressive educator who prizes the well-being of children and youth while seeking ways to counter existing antihumane, test-driven school policies and advance social justice. He wants to subvert traditional schooling because the prevailing ideas that drive the existing system squelch what he prizes.

A former teacher, a director of a school-within-a-school, a principal of and later a teacher in a charter school, and now a professor, Nehring's book falls within the particular genre of those progressive educators who write about public schools. One group scorns public schools for killing creative thinking and reproducing awful socioeconomic structures that strangle the quest for equity. It rejects traditional schooling completely and offers alternative visions of "good" schools constructed outside the current system. Other progressive groups see the public schools as mindlessly hurting all children but especially the powerless poor. But instead of rejecting the system outright, they push for positive changes within the existing schools and classrooms. This book joins the latter group.

So Nehring has not written a woe-is-us screed against the current standards-driven, test-based system of schooling; he has written a we-can-do-better-if-we-see-clearly-what-we-are-up-against book. Drawing from his personal experience in teaching and administering schools and using his research-based knowledge of the history of school reforms, he offers readers five case studies of schools that went against the tide: Bronson Alcott's Temple School in the 1830s, Quincy (Massachusetts) schools in the 1870s, the Beaver Country Day School since the 1920s, his experiences in a school-within-a-school that he and other teachers created in the early 1990s, and a charter school in which he taught and led in the late 1990s. Fascinating in their own right and strongly linked to the themes of the book, the cases illustrate what this passionate progressive wants practitioners to do (and not do) in their classrooms, schools, and district offices.

Nehring lays out a map for "mindful practitioners" to crack the "mindless adoption" of traditional practices in district offices, schools, and classrooms that squelch students' inquiry, creativity, and desire to learn. The gift he offers readers is in these five case studies, his analysis of which dominant ideas glue together a system unfriendly to progressive teaching and learning and practical advice for teachers and administrators to unglue those ideas and become "mindful practitioners." Swimming upstream, Nehring knows, is never easy, but the work of educating the young is so important that it must be done even in the face of "mindless" traditional structures and practices.

Nehring's well-written and highly personal book raises serious questions about how much longer inhumane and counterproductive school policies and practices that suppress student inquiry and creativity can dominate a society rife with inequalities. Whether readers agree or disagree with Nehring, his historical cases, analysis, and advice will excite and provoke them, and that is precisely what he seeks to do.

Larry Cuban

Acknowledgments

At the Beaver Country Day School, I would like to thank Peter Hutton, who granted me generous access to the Beaver Country Day School archives, Maura Power, who welcomed me on my many visits and provided me with office space to review archival materials, and Peter Gow, whose knowledge of the school's history is extensive. In Quincy, my thanks go to the Thomas Crane Public Library staff, who pointed me to numerous valuable sources and entrusted me with archival material. My thanks go also to the Fitchburg State College Library staff for making available to me material from their rare books collection and for keeping the store open late into the night. I would also like to thank Linda Griffin, Bob Sinclair, Joyce Berkman, and Ted Sizer, who carefully read early material that became the basis for this book. I am grateful to the faculty and trustees of the Parker School for their imagination and dedication in establishing an extraordinarily student-centered school. My thanks go as well to the faculty, students, parents, and community members whose courage, imagination, and determination led to the creation of the Bethlehem Lab School, in particular, Jane King, Les Loomis, Pam Williams, Hal Williams, Judy Wooster, and Jon Hunter.

Most of all, I thank my father, who inspires confidence. I am blessed to be his son.

INTRODUCTION

A Conspiracy Theory

I need time to think. So do you. If we don't get it, we end up doing stupid stuff. People who spend their days in schools—the adults and the kids—need time to think, but, by and large, we don't get much of it.

The press of time in schools is well documented, and anyone who has ever spent a day in school as a student or an adult knows firsthand what the research corroborates. The thoughtless practices that result from the press for time are also well documented. Here, too, any parent who has pulled a week's worth of worksheets from her or his child's backpack knows the completely unnecessary tedium this child must endure and the absence of thoughtfulness in so much instructional practice. Popular movies lampooning the foolishness that goes on inside schools sting us not because they are untrue but because they strike so close to the mark.

It is sad and hugely ironic that *the* public institution purporting to develop the life of the mind offers so little time to think. If we are looking for ways to transform instructional practice and, through it, to reform public schooling in this country, then we need look no farther to begin the work than this looming and unfortunate fact. And to truly understand our present condition, we need to examine its deep roots in our national history and culture. This book suggests that, first and foremost, what is missing from American public education are habits of inquiry and reflection, and that the most important step in reforming schooling in the United States is to cultivate among all of us directly engaged in schooling—teachers, school administrators, students—the regular habit of asking good questions about what we are doing and why.

Why is thoughtful practice so elusive in schools? The pursuit of that question takes us, through this book, on an exciting journey from the past to the present, illuminating the origins of our present dilemma and providing us with the knowledge necessary to begin to bring about real and positive change. The plan for this book is simple. First, it names the forces that stand in the way of thoughtful schooling. Second, it explains the origins, behavior, and full dimension of these forces by showing them in action in five representative cases drawn from the past and present. Of equal importance, it tells how, in each case, thoughtful, committed school reformers succeeded in creating and sustaining their vision of school as a place where children and the adults who work with them make inquiry and reflection the chief activity of the day—every day. Third, the book pulls together learning from each case, against the backdrop of our contemporary educational system, offering practical suggestions to educators who wish to bring about positive change.

The Enemy, Named

It is a kind of conspiracy; a conspiracy against thoughtful schooling. Like other conspiracies, it is hidden in plain view, but unlike most conspiracies, the conspirators are not a specific group of individuals, nor do they all come from a particular political party, social movement, religious perspective, or ideology. They cross party lines and religious and ideological boundaries. They are woven into the fabric of our culture, which means they are everywhere. They come from and through each of us. It is a conspiracy of deeply embedded cultural beliefs that we all, to a greater or lesser degree, share. The enemy is us.

The conspiracy must be acknowledged and understood; only then can we begin to address it—as we find it both inside us and wherever it manifests itself in the environment. Whenever we see these forces "out there," at work in the wider world, before we offer some sharp-tongued criticism, we would do well to examine our own habits and dispositions and begin by addressing the conspiracy inside each of us.

This book begins by naming the conspirators, none of which will likely surprise you; but seeing them together, we may begin to understand the deep sources of the central pedagogical problem that all schools face. In order to disarm this conspiracy, we must understand how it operates. This means taking the long view and seeing how, in widely different contexts and historical moments, the six conspirators named here surface again and again to do their insidious work.

Six Conspirators against Thoughtful Schooling

Before going any farther, let's name them. Who are the conspirators? The conspiracy against thoughtful schooling is made up of six and includes, as well, numerous, lesser co-conspirators, such as you and me. We are all fully indictable. Below is the list, laid out here in broad terms. We will move to a much deeper level as our work in this book proceeds.

1. *The manufacturing metaphor:* From the dawn of the Industrial Revolution, the means and ends of industrial manufacturing have influenced to greater or lesser degrees the means and ends of schooling. Over 100 years ago,

industrial manufacturing established a framework of understanding economic production so compelling that we quickly began to apply it to other aspects of culture, failing to acknowledge its logical limits and the potentially harmful consequences of its misuses. The history of public schooling in the United States may be understood as the tragic misapplication of industrial thinking to human growth and learning. That we continue to conceive of schools in terms of industry even in a *post*-industrial society speaks to the enduring power of the manufacturing metaphor to make satisfying (if ultimately disastrous) sense of the world. The problem is that widgets don't think and people do. Widgets are inert. Children live and breathe—a truth as simple as it is overlooked. The day that school committeemen (and they were men) of the nineteenth century began to naively draw comparisons between the red brick buildings in town that produced boots and guns and the red brick buildings that "produced" children was the day that an educational Rubicon was crossed. And as children, increasingly, during the closing decades of the nineteenth century and the early decades of the twentieth century, were organized like parts in a factory, age graded, processed through standardized curricula, shuttled from room to room for fastening on this set of facts and the other set of facts, and as their teachers became laborers responsible for an ever-narrower set of tasks, all parties to the work—pupils and their teachers—were expected to think less and fall in line more. It didn't matter that all the fastened-on facts, like parts, fell off as soon as the product was out the showroom door. What mattered was the process itself, which *looked like* the great and worthy production method of the factory. It made sense there; surely it made good sense here too. Unfortunately, the process has stripped schools of time and, with it, the capacity for thoughtful practice. Imagine: the enemy is a metaphor! This is a correctible error, and it begins by exposing the manufacturing metaphor and rooting our thinking in language and contexts that promote more thoughtful policies, practices, and habits.

2. *The fear factor:* The dual capacity of the human psyche to operate from a standpoint of fear or hope is readily apparent in religious communities, political movements, and parenting styles. Our own experiences of day-to-day life bear out the continual vacillation between the two poles. The cultural climate of a given historical moment can be broadly understood in terms of sources of fear and hopefulness present in the collective consciousness. The legitimacy of both impulses is apparent in our evolution as a species. Both fear and hope are adaptive traits in the right moment. However, they are dangerously maladaptive in the wrong moment. Much in the history of schooling in the United States may be explained by the sources of fear that have driven school policies and instructional practice; whether it is fear of the power of Satan or the idleness of children, fear of the immigrant masses or the angry oppressed races, fear of the enemy, fear of economic competitors, fear of communism, witches, a multicultural society, or maybe just the many lively, intelligent children compressed into an enclosed

space. Fear makes us clamp down, assert control, and insist on compliance and obedience. Time to think for those from whom we seek obedience threatens our ability to control them, therefore, we cut out "idle" time, which means we cut out time to think. We forcibly erode opportunities for thoughtful instructional practice. Fear, while a legitimate and necessary impulse in the right moment, has come to so dominate schooling that, from an evolutionary standpoint, we are threatening our very existence as a species by robbing our offspring of the time and opportunity to develop that capacity that has allowed us as a species to thrive: our ability to think. What are we so afraid of? That is a question to regularly ask ourselves and those with whom we work.

3. *The View from the Top:* In Dilbert cartoons, everything always makes perfect organizational sense to that famously clueless manager with the pointy hair. But the workers in their cubicles know that whatever the manager cooks up actually will make no sense at all in the workplace. What makes the cartoon so funny is how confident and how wrong the manager is. Dilbert appeals to us because we have all had the frustrating experience of recognizing the stupidity at ground level of policies directed from up high with such swift certainty. And while most of us value sound support and guidance from above, we all legitimately rail against directives that we must carry out contrary to our better judgment. The history of American schooling could unfortunately be drawn as a series of very funny (and very sad) Dilbert cartoons, with the cluelessness and power of the pointy-haired man growing ever more dire as we progress toward the present. But the pointy-haired man is us. He represents the impulse to create a tidy plan in order to serve our own psychological satisfaction instead of the needs and abilities of those impacted by it. The pointy-haired man is the worst sort of bureaucracy, the off-the-shelf school reform "model" ready to be "implemented." It is the teacher-proof curriculum, the kid-proof lesson plan, the endless conveyor belt of classroom worksheets, and the endless lists of what children should know, annually produced by state commissions, congressional committees, scholars, and school committees. It is the notion that good schools may be "replicated." It is "professional development" by the consultant who blows in, blows hard, and blows out. And in all these cases, it is the systematic theft of the opportunity to think for those whose thinking, thoughtfully deployed, would powerfully enhance their own learning. We ought to regularly ask, does this practice or that policy or this curriculum or that school reform model really enhance instructional practice, or does it just look nice from afar?

4. *The Grand Interlock.* My brother converted his aging, diesel-powered Mercedes, at one point, to run on vegetable oil. He made some small modifications to the fuel delivery system, installed a secondary fuel tank in the trunk, and was able to power his car without drawing down our planet's dwindling supply of fossil fuels and without polluting the air. It was a great innovation. Unfortunately, there were no commercial vendors within 100 miles of his home to provide

vegetable oil in the quantity, quality, and price range appropriate to running his car. Undeterred by this fact, my brother regularly made the rounds of the local restaurants in his town asking if he might take away the waste cooking oil, usually standing in a big drum by the dumpster out back. He then transported it home, filtered it, stored it, and poured twenty gallons of it into his auxiliary gas tank whenever it started to run low. This was a lot of work, which he was willing to do. But how long might he be willing to keep doing it? Moreover, as marvelous as this innovation is, without easily available fueling stations, how likely is it the idea will ever catch on beyond a few determined environmentalists with good mechanical skills and lots of patience? Not likely. Unfortunately, the system is just not set up for it. What the system *is* set up for are vehicles that consume a finite and dwindling natural resource while spewing dangerous chemicals into the atmosphere. I tell this story of innovation in automobile fuel because it is analogous to so many innovations in education. Like my brother's veggie car, many innovations in school practice make marvelous sense, offering notable gains in student growth and learning, often through a more thoughtful use of time, but they never catch on because the system is not set up to support them. And while they may flourish under the devoted care of a committed few, exhaustion eventually prevails, and the innovation fades. And like the world of automobiles, even though the larger system is deeply problematic, the system is just so enormous and interlocking that it is incapable of change. In the logic of the system, it matters less where the whole thing is headed and more how all the parts function together. It is both magnificent and ridiculous, an elegant catastrophe. The question we need to ask here, when we find practices that actually enhance learning, is this: Where will this innovation collide with the gears of the larger system, and how may we fashion a workable interface?

5. *The Politics of Appeasement:* The natural desire to please entices us to say yes to all who petition us with legitimate concerns. In schools, we wish to say yes to all the legitimate demands to add this goal or that piece of curriculum for some very good reason. As appropriate as this may feel in any given moment, the collective weight of all this yes-saying is sinking the ship of public education. Our schools possess finite resources, the chief of which is time. Making ever more demands on the time we have leads to a crowded plan. And like a one-hour meeting with a five- hour agenda, it makes everyone crazy and stupid. We end up doing nothing well. In fact, it is *not* a virtue to say yes to all, it is a failure of valuing the work. It is a corruption that comes from a fear of engaging in difficult conversations about the deeper purposes of schooling. Whenever we are asked to add, we must be in the habit of also asking, where will we subtract? Better yet, we should be in the habit of asking, where may we subtract goals and requirements in order to slim down the agenda to a manageable size, a size at which good work may be accomplished and thoughtful instructional practice may be unleashed?

6. *The failure of generosity and justice.* When our oldest daughter was a sophomore in high school, we made a family decision for her to attend an expensive, private boarding school for her final two years of secondary schooling. We are public school folk, and the public school she was attending was a marvelous place, and until then, we had never imagined that a private prep school would be a part of any of our children's school experience. But for a host of compelling personal reasons, including the fact that she was a very promising visual artist, she went off to boarding school and we cleaned out our bank accounts. We did this for two reasons: because we love our daughter and because we could. Sure, we complained about the cost and the impact on our modest assets, but in the end it was doable. How many other parents face circumstances in which their child would benefit from a different educational setting and yet are unable, through lack of money or know-how, to make a change? The answer: millions. If I were to invite any parent living in urban poverty to take a ride with me to visit the school my daughter attended and said your child may attend here too, if you wish, what are the chances they would say no to the warm, nurturing environment, the beautifully landscaped campus, the small classes, the relaxed pace, and the combination of academic rigor and individual support? Slim to none. There is something fundamentally unfair about the fact that I can do this for my daughter and so many others cannot, especially in the richest country in the world, and especially in a democracy. The truth is, we take care of our own the best way we can. The problem is that the best way I can, because of my relative privilege as a white, well-educated, middle-class, heterosexual male, is far better than the best way that many other parents in the United States can. It's as unfair as it is true. If we all cared as much about other people's children as we do about our own, and expressed that commitment in our public policies, then education would be utterly transformed. That we do not as a republic ensure that all children have access to high-quality education is a failure of vision, a failure of generosity, and a failure of justice. We ought to be asking, would I consent to subject my own children to the consequences of any given practice or policy? Moreover, would I *want* it for my child?

Learning from the Long View Back

In the book ahead, we take a fascinating look at five schools from different historical periods, and we will see how our conspirators, regardless of the decade or the century, do their work. We will also learn from people long ago (and not so long ago) who ingeniously thwarted the conspirators, and, for a time at least, cultivated thoughtful practice in schools and classrooms.

But first I want to tell a short, personal story that I hope will persuade you of the value of our excursion into the past. Some years ago, I wrote a book about my experience founding and directing a small alternative high school near Albany, New York. The book was published and reviewed. One review appeared in the Canadian Journal *Curriculum Inquiry*. The review was written by the eminent education historian Larry Cuban. Professor Cuban wrote that while the book was well written, its perspective was "limited and short-sighted."[1] Cuban pointed out that in writing my book, I seemed totally unaware of the generations of school reformers before me who had made similar efforts and founded schools and movements with similar aspirations. He implied that if school reformers, including me, became more informed about such efforts, we might be more effective in initiating and sustaining our own school reform undertakings. At first I was upset by what struck me as a "bad review." With time, though, my heart softened to Professor Cuban's criticism, and I admitted he was right. That's when I decided to go back to graduate school to study the history of progressive education. Five years later, I earned my doctorate, with a dissertation focusing on several progressive schools and a new trajectory for my professional life. I would undertake to make sense of the forces that work against thoughtful schooling and to try to help others succeed in their efforts to establish thoughtful schools. This book represents where that journey has taken me so far.

What changed my own thinking so powerfully, as I began to read about previous efforts, was to observe the forces against thoughtful schooling at work across so many different situations during so many different eras. Reading a school committee report from 100 years ago that discusses per pupil spending and the deadening impact of state tests on learning was shockingly familiar. Reading about the criticism that a school leader in Boston faced for placing too much emphasis on "analysis" and too little on content was striking not so much because it was familiar (which it was), but because it happened nearly 200 years ago!

Where these moments of recognition tended to occur was not in my readings of the sweeping historical surveys found in history textbooks but in the examination of actual documents, yellowed and crumbling (or on microfilm) from real schools where courageous school leaders were taking a stand against stupidity. Here I found comfort and inspiration knowing others had gone before me. And here I gained valuable insight into the successful means—of use in any era—by which savvy school leaders have beaten the odds, created an opening in the system, and held on at least for a period of time. In this book,it is my purpose to grant you the same experience I had, finding comfort, inspiration, and insight from an exploration of the past and cultivating our own confidence in knowing which questions to ask and which moves to make in similar circumstances today.

The Thinking behind the Book

The theoretical source for the conspirators named in this book is the empirical evidence of the five schools. In identifying the five schools examined here, I sought places at the edge of the mainstream that pushed against it and stood a promising chance of holding their own, at least for a time. My persistent question in reviewing sources and assembling the narrative of each school was, what are the forces that have worked for and against thoughtful practice in each school? I did not enter the study with a theory. My goal was to ground whatever findings might accrue in the evidence as it presented itself.

What I have chosen to call conspirators are the themes that emerge from my examination of the individual and collective record of these schools. Other lesser themes, identified in individual chapters, also appear, but their echo across schools and across the landscape of American education, as I understand it, is less resonant.

It may be asked whether the themes named here are rooted in American culture or ultimately in human psychology. That is an entirely appropriate question for further study. My focus has been to identify the themes that spring from the record of these five schools. Because they are embedded in American culture, I have described them as such. But whether they may be found in other cultures and find a common origin in human psychology or some other anthropological universality is for others to pursue. I suspect the fear factor has psychological roots, for example. The manufacturing metaphor may be found in other societies where public schooling was coemergent with industrial manufacturing. It may also be asserted that five other schools might yield five different themes. That may also be true. I won't vouch for the presence or absence of other historically rooted tendencies in American schooling. Additional studies may indeed augment or refine the ideas presented here. The ones presented here, however, are powerful. Understanding their origins and applying that knowledge to contemporary manifestations of them in our own school practice will enhance opportunities for student learning and yield more thoughtful schools.

I certainly entered the study with my own biases: the bias of a school practitioner who eschews overintellectualization; the bias of a philosophical pragmatist in the James and Dewey tradition, which means that, epistemologically, I lean toward valuing propositions according to their practical consequences; and the bias of a constructivist who believes that whatever meaning we make in the world is highly context-bound and subject to continual revision.

Six Fascinating Tales

This book is a hybrid of history and personal experience. It draws on stories constructed from the historical record and lived accounts from contemporary school reform. It is also a deliberately focused book, looking, as if through a telescope, at a few small stars in a heaven of bright lights, based on a belief that we may learn more about stars by looking up close at one or two than by staring wide-eyed at the entire night sky.

We move, then, to the five schools. Although they are all responsive in some way to the six conspirators, each one is especially responsive to one or two of them. Conveniently, for us, then, the book ahead focuses on one conspirator at a time by looking closely at that school which most interestingly took it on. With each chapter focusing on one of the conspirators, we are able to identify lessons that school reformers today may learn from our predecessors. Each chapter also includes three contemporary scenarios that will illuminate the practical application of learning from each case. One scenario, called "Classroom Encounters," addresses the ways in which we as teachers in our classrooms encounter and may overcome the cultural conspirators. A second scenario, called "Teacher Talk," addresses the ways in which the conspirators surface in our collegial interactions as well as the ways in which we, as a profession, may counter them. A third scenario, called "Public Engagement," focuses on our interactions as educators with the public at large and how we may address the cultural conspiracy against thoughtful practice that surfaces in public conversation. A final chapter in the book is devoted to the collective learning we may draw from these six tales.

Chapter 1, "The Manufacturing Metaphor," asks: How do you overcome the deeply embedded cultural tendency to view schools as businesses, and, most often, manufacturing centers, that is, factories? To gain insight into this question, we begin by looking at two thoughtful school leaders and the successful steps they took to hold the manufacturing metaphor at bay, even though the schools they led were situated in the heart of a manufacturing community, surrounded by other school systems that were enamored with the manufacturing metaphor.

Most people regard John Dewey as the father of progressive education, but Dewey would disagree. He once said that the honor goes rightly to a man named Francis W. Parker. Though Parker's name is no longer current in educational philosophy discussions, during the latter part of the nineteenth century he was the school innovator of the day, written about as widely as Grant Wiggins or Parker Palmer. The five years Francis Parker spent as superintendent of the Quincy, Massachusetts, schools, showed that even when surrounded by factories in the thick of the Industrial Revolution, educators could successfully assert that children are not widgets, and that schools, and the people in them, may thoughtfully prevail over the manufacturing metaphor.

Chapter 2, "The Fear Factor," relates a cautionary tale, offering numerous lessons for us today about the importance of understanding the prevailing cultural balance between fear and hope in establishing and sustaining thoughtful school practices. When Louisa May Alcott, author of *Little Women,* was still a girl, her father, Bronson Alcott, was a rising figure in New England schooling.

In 1834, he founded a small school on Tremont Street in Boston in which the focus was thoughtful examination of issues through discussion and reflective writing. Alcott boldly defied dominant school practice rooted in the Puritan fear of the evil in human hearts and the dangers of idle children. For a short time, the school flourished, an amazing accomplishment from which we may learn some lessons still applicable today. But rapidly, the school fell out of favor with the city's leaders and met a spectacular demise in which Mr. Alcott could have lost his life at the hands of an unruly mob.

Chapter 3, "The View from the Top," moves us from history to the present, as I discuss the birth and early years of a public charter school with which I was personally associated. The Francis W. Parker Charter Essential School, from its inception, stood the norms of bureaucratic organization on their head and created a school culture committed to one kid at a time and instructional practice rooted in thoughtful attention to each student. Here are powerful lessons for any public school today—whether charter or district-based—about the mind-set needed to nurture thoughtful school practice.

Chapter 4, "The Grand Interlock," focuses on a school with which I have been associated. It is the school about which I previously wrote, for which Larry Cuban correctly tagged me as naïve and myopic. In this chapter, I revisit the story of this school, identifying the ways in which it wrestled with the larger system that enveloped it, chronicling both its successes and shortcomings. As a school-within-a-school, the Bethlehem Lab School illustrates the crucial importance of developing workable interfaces between innovative practice and the indifferent gears of the larger system.

Chapter 5, "The Politics of Appeasement," discusses the Beaver Country Day School. Public school folk (myself included) have been known to dismiss the private school world because it is elitist. But we ignore such schools at our peril, for the elite private schools of this country show us just how good school can be when the conspirators against thoughtful schooling are held at bay by a combination of money and power. They also suggest strategies that public schools might adopt that are not the exclusive domain of privilege. The Beaver Country Day School, founded when the progressive education movement was at its zenith, is a prime example of what a school can be when all the right forces are in alignment and a school is able to establish and maintain a clear and persuasive mission. Here we see a school that drew uncompromisingly on the learning of the progressive era. Here, too, we observe a school that drifted from its mooring in an effort to reach out to more and more students. How this school began, how it lost its way, and how it found itself again provide lessons to private and public school people alike.

Chapter 6, "The Failure of Generosity and Justice," focuses on the ways in which each school has sought diligently to achieve the ideals of generosity and justice, and how each school has also fallen short. This conspirator is so pervasive across our culture and our history that no one school featured in this book has felt it any less powerfully than the others.

Chapter 7, "The Mindful Practitioner," pulls together the many lessons of the past and present that emerge as themes from these representative cases, in the context of the larger system in which they are embedded, and offers some practical suggestions for effective ways to take on the conspirators and liberate our schools for our children and their teachers. While every school setting is different, if your school is located in the United States, then you are unavoidably bound up in the culture that is the focus of this book, and you are subject to the silent conspiracy against thoughtful practice in your school. More importantly, armed with the deep understanding this book offers, you, too, can prevail over the larger culture and create a thoughtful learning environment wherever you may be.

1

The Manufacturing Metaphor

Framing the Issue

Jonathan Kozol, in *The Shame of the Nation: The Restoration of Apartheid Schooling in America*, his critique of American public education, writes of the contemporary influence of big business in school curriculum and instruction.[1] Kozol insightfully documents the ways in which business thinking narrows the curriculum and diminishes learning opportunities for children. This sad reality would be unfortunate enough if it were a recent phenomenon, but it is not. Business thinking has dominated American public schooling since at least the dawn of the Industrial Revolution. As Kozol illuminates its contemporary form, historians David Tyack and Larry Cuban, in their seminal work, *Tinkering toward Utopia: A Century of Public School Reform*, track it through the decades of the twentieth century, naming its various incarnations.[2]

Despite its harmful effects, business thinking, or, what we will call the manufacturing metaphor, has dominated discourse about public schooling for decades, and it continues unabated. The challenge for contemporary school leaders, as has been the challenge for many years, is to, somehow, effectively shift the language of schools to terms that are more appropriate to the learning of children and more constructive to the pursuit of public education in a democratic society.

To gain insight into this challenge, we begin by looking at two thoughtful school leaders and the successful steps they take to hold the manufacturing metaphor at bay, even though the schools they lead are situated in the heart of a manufacturing community, surrounded by other school systems and a state bureaucracy that are enamored with the manufacturing metaphor. As contemporary as these issues may feel, the "case in point" that focuses this chapter falls in the late nineteenth century. The story that follows, in almost all ways, could be the tale of a modern school system, maybe one just like yours. The fact that it took place over 100 years ago allows us to see the *whole* story from beginning to end. Such omniscience, impossible in the schools we inhabit today, since their stories are yet unfolding, is one of the great attractions of history as a source of knowledge about contemporary challenges. We get to see how it turned out for others, thereby allowing us to avoid their mistakes and build on their successes.

Case in Point

For an extended moment in the 1870s and 1880s, a powerfully thoughtful impulse took hold of the Quincy, Massachusetts, schools. At a time when Boston schools and those of the communities within its orbit were succumbing to the intellectually numbing forces of mechanization and mass production, the schools of Quincy managed to resist the gravitational pull and, for a period, provided the pupils in their care with a nurturing and an intellectually stimulating environment.

Why, at a time when public schools were sadly falling in line with the industrial machine, did Quincy buck the trend? What are the forces that helped sustain the Quincy movement for as long as it lasted? What are the forces that tended to erode it? Finally, what implications do events in Quincy relatively long ago carry for contemporary school leaders seeking to infuse schools and school systems with thoughtful instructional practice and improved learning opportunities for their students?

The Adams family (of presidential renown) was, throughout the nineteenth century, a powerful force in local Quincy affairs where their family home stood. In the 1870s, their energies converged on the School Committee, with elder brother John Quincy Adams Jr. serving as chairman and younger brother Charles Francis Adams Jr. winning election to the committee in 1872. The event that seems to have catalyzed the Adams's interest in the schools beyond merely overseeing them in the accustomed patrician manner was a new examination system established by fellow committeeman Henry Farnum Smith. In 1872, Smith proposed that the School Committee assume direct control of the end-of-term oral examination of students, formerly conducted by teachers. The impetus for this action seems to have been a general disappointment among committee members with the poor performance of students in their school exhibitions.

The committee's new policy was essentially an end run around the teaching staff, and committee members seem to have taken some delight in the procedure. In the memoir of a teacher who worked in Quincy at that time, we learn "how the Adamses seemed to enjoy questioning pupils in American history, when they found any able to think and to express what they know in an original, natural manner. But oh, what frowns were cast on the class when most of them answered in single words or in the stilted sentences of the text-book."[3]

But committee members were not merely interested in outmaneuvering the teachers or catching students performing poorly. They sought, rather, to infuse the school system with a habit of original thought. Their dismay at rote "text-book" answers was therefore great.

Smith's examination system gave the committee members a direct window on student learning and confirmed what they had suspected about the poor quality of education in the school system. Their lack of enthusiasm for the school system's work comes across in the annual report they submitted in 1873:

> A retrospect of ten years will discover no very remarkable results. Ten years ago, so far as we remember, the children read and wrote and spelled about as well as they do to-day; and the fundamental rules of arithmetic were as thoroughly taught then as now. And at present, as in the past, most of the pupils who have finished the grammar course neither speak nor spell their own language very perfectly, nor read and write it with that elegance which is desirable. This immobility seems to show that a point has been reached which is near the natural term of such force as our present system of schooling is calculated to exert.[4]

In contemporary terms, we would say that the Quincy School Committee was after transformative change, that is, not merely improvement of outcomes for existing standards but a whole new set of standards on which to base student learning.

The true depth of their disappointment, not only with the Quincy schools but Massachusetts common schools in general, is signaled unreservedly by Charles Adams in a retrospective essay he composed several years later. "The school year has become one long period of diffusion and cram, the object of which is to successfully pass a stated series of examinations. This leads directly to superficiality. Smatter is the order of the day."[5] Adams's lament could easily be uttered, verbatim, by any principal or superintendent today faced with the strictures of the No Child Left Behind Act (NCLB) and the standardized testing mania that it is breeding in our schools.

If "superficiality" and "smatter" were the order of the day, then Charles Adams claimed to know where such thinking came from, namely, the mechanistic, highly centralized, batch process mentality of his increasingly industrial society, "the last new theory, so curiously amplified in some of our larger cities, that vast numbers of children should be taught as trains on a railroad are run, on a time-table principle,—that they are here now, that they will be at such another point to-morrow, and at their terminus at such a date;—while a general superintendent sits in his central office and pricks off each step in the advance of the whole line on a chart before him . . ."[6]

How familiar this all sounds to the contemporary ear! Substitute the railroad metaphor with the top-down accountability movement currently in vogue with the Federal Department of Education and its counterparts at the state level and everything else fits: children taught on a timetable principle, vast numbers of them expected to all be at the same place at the same moment, while the commissioners of education sit in their central office pricking off each step!

Adams's reference to railroads was no casual allusion, as he had spent ten years (1869–1879) as a railroad commissioner for Massachusetts.[7] He was well acquainted with the industry. What is curious is that, contrary to many leaders of his day, he did not adopt the ethos of clocklike efficiency, mechanization, and centralized control so essential to the rail industry as the guiding ethos for social/institutional organization in general or for schooling in particular. In contemporary terms, it would be as if the chairman of the board of Wal-Mart stores said that schools should not in any way emulate the business model advanced by Wal-Mart. Although "clocklike efficiency" was, for Adams, a reasonable way to run a railroad, it was not a reasonable way to organize a school.

This conscious distancing from the industrial method says much about who Adams was. Though situated historically in the full current of the Industrial Revolution, his psyche seems to have been rooted in a preindustrial, eighteenth-century, agrarian America. While he acknowledged and even admired the power and efficiency of the factory system and the railroad in the production and distribution of goods, he seems wisely to have drawn a line between the ways of nineteenth-century commerce and the means of good schooling. Although most of us who work in schools today did not grow up on farms or in rural, pastoral settings, we can still draw on the agrarian metaphors that guided Adams's way of thinking about education. With our modern knowledge of ecology, we can more deeply appreciate the notions of interdependence, complexity, and developmentalism that both the preindustrial, agrarian worldview and a contemporary ecological worldview support. (We will say more about this later.)

Not surprisingly, Adams's view of the world in this regard stood at odds with that of most school committee members of his day. All around him, school committees, peopled most often by white men who led local businesses, fully embraced centralization, bureaucracy, clock-based efficiency, and orderliness not just as values in the industrial workplace but as ideals for their schools as well. To such men striving to be "modern," the values and practices of the industrial workplace were the wave of the future and needed as quickly as possible to be adopted by all social institutions, including the schools.

Again, how utterly familiar that school board members, who work by day in organizations guided largely by business practices, would suggest with knowing authority that, *of course, this is how one should also run a school.* The corollary also applies: *It's no wonder the school is failing, since it is not being guided by sound business principles!* And the corollary of the corollary applies too: *What this place needs is a good CEO to come in and bust heads!*

Adams and his older brother did not share this view. There existed, therefore, the possibility that if thoughtful leadership emerged within the schools, it would not be sabotaged and, indeed, might find warm support from the local school committee. Such leadership appeared serendipitously in the person of Francis W. Parker.

In 1875, the School Committee advertised for the newly created position of "superintendent" of the Quincy schools. The notion of a superintendency had grown increasingly popular in the Massachusetts schools of the time, and the Adamses, while not embracing the industrial order as the means to good schooling, nonetheless saw merit in the idea of a hired expert to organize the schools. Parker, recently returned from university study in Berlin and jobless, answered the ad in person and immediately impressed the School Committee, which had been unimpressed with previous candidates.[8] He was quickly hired and became the first superintendent of the Quincy schools.

There was a strong compatibility between Charles Adams and Francis Parker. Both were from old- line Yankee stock, and both appeared to have been psychically rooted in a rural, agrarian America. Although Adams was a blue blood, while Parker had grown up in relative poverty in New Hampshire, they had come to a similar place in their feelings about schools. Charles Adams, schooled at Boston Latin and Harvard, imagined that schooling ought to be conducted in the way he had experienced it, and that the results in the schoolchildren should be similar too. This meant small classes with lots of individual attention, capable teachers, and a pedagogy that nurtured the intellect. Parker, influenced by his own experiences as a young schoolmaster in New Hampshire and Ohio, had discovered early that children respond better to lessons that appeal to their curiosity and humor and are rooted in their own experiences. He found his instincts affirmed in his studies in Berlin, where it is likely that he read Pestalozzi and Froebel.

The strength of the alignment between the Adamses and Parker is borne out by the success of Parker's first major policy move as superintendent in 1876, which was, surprisingly, to *shorten* the school year. Upon his inspection of the schools, he had become concerned by the level of truancy. While he could have chosen to hire more truancy officers and stiffen the penalty for unexcused school absences, he instead reasoned that pupils were weary from a school term that wore on longer than they could endure. He, therefore, shortened the school year from forty-three to forty weeks and created a trimester school year. Just imagine, a superintendent of a medium-size city today suggesting that students might learn better if the required days of attendance were reduced! It clearly makes no sense if one's assumption is that seat time equals educational achievement—the more time your butt is in a chair, the more knowledge your head will fill up with. The longer you run the production process, the more parts you can fasten onto the frame. While this, sadly, is the dominant ethos in our own times, with strident calls for a longer school day, a longer school year, less recess, and more "time on task," Parker's thinking was driven by a different set of assumptions. Among these were (1) children who are tired will not learn well; (2) learning seeded in schools may germinate and grow while children are elsewhere. This was not to dismiss the importance of time as an important factor in school organization. It was, rather, to understand it rightly among the full array of factors that ought to be considered in the equation that is school.

Thus Superintendent Parker reported in his first Annual Report to the School Committee in early 1876, "The shortening of the school year, and its division into three terms, with vacations at the close of each, has, I think, remedied this difficulty [truancy] . . ."[9] This single act and its warm acceptance by the School Committee are an extraordinary signal of the progressive instincts that drove both Parker and his committee. This was not a superintendent who wanted his workers at the factory for extended hours; Parker was, rather, an individual who understood children and sought to enhance their learning through an appeal to their developmental needs. A sharp rise in average daily attendance, which in 1874 hovered at 77 percent and by 1876 had rocketed to 95 percent, suggests that the innovation was having a positive impact.[10] Such data suggest, too, that even in terms of "time on task," Parker's solution was effective, since the number of days actually attended by children during his shortened school year exceeded the number of days attended under the previous (longer) school year.

Improved attendance may have been due also to changes in classroom instruction, which Parker inspired in his teachers. Parker's pedagogy did not embrace the industrial metaphor for learning, that is, a product assembly approach in which facts and subjects are attached to the child's mind (understood as inert) like parts to a frame. Instead, children were rightly understood to possess intelligence and imagination. Charles Adams reported the following:

The old "dame school" disappeared at once. In place of it appeared something as different as light from darkness. The alphabet itself was no longer taught. In place of the old, lymphatic, listless "school marm," pressing into the minds of tired and listless children the mystic significance of certain hieroglyphics by mere force of over-laying, as it were,—instead of this time-honored machine-process, young women, full of life and nervous energy, found themselves surrounded at the blackboard with groups of little ones who were learning how to read almost without knowing it;—learning how to read, in a word, exactly as they had before learned how to speak, not by rule and rote and by piecemeal, but altogether and by practice.[11]

Straying farther still from the industrial ideal, Parker also altered student promotion policy to reflect the individualistic pace of student growth. Doing away with once-a-year exams, students were encouraged to demonstrate readiness for the next level at any time. Parker wrote in the 1876 report to the School Committee, "Pupils are promoted whenever it is found, by examination, that they are well fitted to do the work of the next class above, without regard to the number of years they have attended school."[12]

In these pedagogical moves, we see how, at the instructional level, as well as the organizational level, Parker, with the Adamses' support, embraced a different way of thinking, a way of thinking attuned to the developmental needs of children, the varying rates of speed at which children show readiness for new concepts, and the organic way in which learning arises from the interface between experience and imagination. It's no wonder John Dewey called Parker the father of progressive education! How many of us who work in schools see children and learning essentially in this way also, and yet we allow ourselves to be overwhelmed by the language and culture of mechanization. We ought to take our cue from Parker, who faced an equal, if not a more potent, mix of mechanistic forces and was determined to rise above them in the interest of authentic learning.

Parker's departure from mechanistic thinking apparently had an enduring impact on the Quincy school system as an analysis of student age by grade level conducted by one of Parker's successors in 1888 (nearly a decade following Parker's departure from Quincy) showed an age range of four to eight years for each grade level from "Primary D" (first year of school), where students ranged from age five to ten, to "First Class," with students as young as fifteen and as old as twenty.[13]

While sensitivity to child development of the sort that Parker demonstrated is crucial to thoughtful schooling, all the sensitivity in the world will come to naught if a school leader fails to attend to public opinion. Long before the Bill Clinton campaign realized "It's about the economy, stupid," Francis Parker recognized that he would be granted enormous running room if he demonstrated tangible restraint in spending the townspeoples' tax dollars.

Sensitive to the overriding budgetary concerns of the community, Parker strategically reduced per pupil spending each of the five years that he presided as superintendent. The School Committee's Report of 1881 shows that spending declined steadily from $23.19 per pupil in 1875 to $20.81 in 1880, Parker's last year.[14]

Budgetary constraints represented possibly Parker's greatest practical challenge to the effective enactment of a thoughtful pedagogy, since close attention to individual pupils requires an ample complement of teachers. The challenge was met with the establishment of a teacher training school, which infused the schools with a cadre of no-cost "assistants." This innovation seems to have resulted in an average class size in the Quincy schools that was markedly less than many of its contemporaries. A superintendent from Lawrence, Massachusetts, commented at a meeting of New England superintendents in 1879 on the "reasonable number of scholars, say 10 or 12, constituting a class" in the Quincy schools, which he compares to "50 or 60 . . . too often the case in New England."[15] A visitor in 1883 corroborates: "normal girls in nearly every room as volunteer assistants."[16] The impact on classroom learning must have been enormously positive, as the student-teacher ratio sank apparently as low as one- fourth of that of other New England school districts. At the same time, the low cost of the "assistants" did not strain the budget.

The popularity of Parker's training school grew with the increasing notoriety of Parker's work, greatly easing the effort to bring in more teachers. B. G. Northrop, secretary of the Connecticut Board of Education, commented in 1883 that "the celebrity given to the [Quincy] schools . . . attracted many pupil-teachers, volunteering to teach that they might thus learn the methods. In this way it was easy to divide each school into small groups of ten or twelve, and secure the constant activity of every child, and an unusual amount of individual teaching."[17]

Contemporary school leaders would do well to note Parker's entrepreneurial behavior, if not the specifics of his solutions. While teacher training may not be the way to reduce class size in every school or district, Parker's strong determination to achieve his vision against what, at the time, must have appeared to be overwhelming obstacles is an inspiration. When we are faced with seemingly insurmountable barriers to thoughtful schooling (NCLB, lock-tight collective bargaining agreements, dysfunctional school boards, etc.), we will do well to consider what we might still do with the hand we are dealt instead of whining about our fate. Though whining is often justified, and sometimes therapeutic, it is rarely constructive.

The success of Parker's efforts seems to have been due in no small measure to Parker's personal charm. One contemporary wrote, "What does he do? How does he do it? He actually superintends,—not by means of reports and blanks and orders from the office, but by being a living presence in every school-room; and, more than that, by being a living power in the thinking of his teachers by his philosophical training-work with them."[18] Another commentator wrote, ". . . we see in Quincy a beautiful development of freedom and inventiveness in the teacher, which comes from the familiar and human way in which these methods are put to them by their superintendent."[19] In fact, contemporary appraisals of Parker create the portrait of a man who was robust, energetic, optimistic, good-humored, and gentle with children—a natural teacher and leader of teachers. As late as 1900, even as Parker's ideas had slipped nationally from the spotlight, a twenty-fifth anniversary celebration of Parker's arrival in Quincy prompted a page-one story in the *Quincy Patriot* that lionized Parker as civil war hero, transformer of classrooms, child prodigy, you name it.[20] The celebration was sponsored not by the School Committee or the municipal government but, interestingly, by the Quincy Teachers Association, bearing testimony to Parker's enduring appeal among the women and men he had led.

Hearing about these charismatic qualities that Parker possessed, some of us might despair that our own tepid "personal charm" falls far short, and that if one of the job requirements for effective leadership is amazing charisma, then we may as well fold up our tent. If it were really about that elusive thing we call charisma, then tent-folding would be exactly the right move, but if we examine the particulars of Parker's actions, what emerges looks less like magic and more like the simple application of sound, widely recognized leadership principles. Consider, for a moment, what Parker actually did. Parker's success with his teachers was due perhaps in part to the departure of those he did not get along with. While school committees of the day seem to have made a habit of complaining about teacher turnover (perhaps as a way of explaining the disappointments they felt with their schools), Quincy also experienced its share of steady turnover throughout Parker's superintendency.[21] Whether teachers were leaving out of dislike for Parker's ways or reasons unrelated, their departure, together with the rising notoriety of the Quincy schools, ensured that with each year, Parker's teachers were ever more enthusiastically behind their leader, as with each year the percentage of the staff personally hired by Parker grew.

Parker was as popular with the community as he was with the teachers. Far more the populist than either of the Adamses could ever hope to be, he was admired by the working-class families of Quincy's stone-cutting industry as a man of humble origin, heroism in battle (he was, after all, a wounded veteran officer of the Civil War), and "hard-knocks" education. His very persona communicated credibility with townspeople, and he was, to at least some extent, active in town affairs outside of the schools.[22]

An additional crucial ingredient in the Quincy success was the promotional work carried out by Charles Adams. An already established public commentator on issues of the day, Adams became a public relations machine for Parker and what he called "the new departure" in Quincy. In the spring of 1879, he presented a speech for the Association of School Committees and Superintendents of Norfolk County, Massachusetts, which was reprinted elsewhere and became widely referenced as "The Quincy Method," gaining a national reputation. The highly influential Adams also saw to it that articles were placed prominently in newspapers in New York, Boston, and Chicago, often writing the articles himself. The *New England Journal of Education*, the leading professional journal of the day, shows fourteen citations for either "Parker, F. W." or "Quincy" during the period 1879–1880. For a single (noncity) school district to attract that many citations in a single publication is remarkable.[23]

Notoriety for the Quincy schools seems to have reached a peak in 1880 and 1881. Some 13,000 visitors observed classes in Quincy's six school buildings in 1881 alone. While visitors remained a regular feature of school life after that, by 1885, the number of visitors had fallen to (a mere!) 5,271.[24]

Parker's departure in 1880 as the Quincy schools were riding the crest of a wave of popularity was prompted by an offer of more money and the likelihood of greater influence as a supervisor in the Boston school system. After five years of stunning success in Quincy, Parker likely felt he had completed a job well done and yearned to move on.

At the heart of the Quincy success was a pedagogy that embraced a humane, organic view of child development that stood starkly at odds with the mechanistic, batch-production mentality of the day. More than a pedagogy, it was a fundamental *anschauung*, asserting that people and human institutions are fundamentally different from widgets and widget production. Adams and Parker together asserted this view from their positions of leadership in both large and small matters, day in and day out. In sum, a liberal idealism prevailed in Quincy against all popular trends due to the presence of a capable, liberal-mindedschool leader who had the backing of a powerful, aristocratic dynasty.

Larger Lessons

Well over 100 years ago, the school leaders of an industrial community prevailed over the dominant industrial mind-set and fashioned schools attuned to the natural learning inclinations of children. Today we face surprisingly similar challenges. How we address these challenges, or fail to, will determine the extent to which our schools and our students are able to grow and flourish. In what follows, we step inside the contemporary dilemmas of three educators as they navigate three different realms—the classroom, the faculty room, and a public meeting. Industrial thinking has made a deep mark at all levels of the system, on our students, on ourselves as educators, and in the public mind. These three scenarios are illustrations, likely all too familiar, of the challenges we face. They also serve as an opportunity to explore how we may counter the dominant culture.

Classroom Encounters

Fresh from a wonderful, inspiring, professional development program, you return to your classroom to try out a new idea. The technique you have learned is designed to elicit student opinions—and their reasoning—on an issue of importance. It takes the figurative question, "Where do you stand?" and gives it literal meaning by having students get up out of their chairs and stand on a line marked across the front of the room, with one end of the line representing one opinion on the issue and the other end representing the opposite opinion (capital punishment is an appropriate consequence for certain crimes; capital punishment is wrong). Students stand at one end or the other or somewhere in between, representing where on the continuum their opinions lie. Volunteers then offer their views and their thinking.

This activity worked marvelously well in the practice session with all of the teachers participating in the workshop. They heard views different from their own, listened respectfully to a range of opinions, and were encouraged to change their positions on the line if they felt "moved" by something someone else said. Your understanding of the issue and your awareness of and sensitivity to your fellow citizens were deepened. You saw how people with divergent views might begin to move toward consensus. New and contextualized knowledge was constructed socially, in the moment. It was a great experience.

Excitedly, you explain the activity to your class, framing the issue and the two opinions represented by the two ends of the continuum. You invite your young charges to come to the front of the room and "take a stand." This is where the activity begins to fall apart. Students are reluctant to get out of their seats. Several eye each other warily, as if to say, you go first, or as if to ask, where are you gonna stand? Slowly, the established opinion leaders rise and move to the front. With defiant looks, the leaders move to places on the line—mostly at the extreme ends—and stamp their feet into position with purpose and preparedness—as if for an assault. Others follow, representing a clear pecking order of social hierarchy within the student culture. Concerned, but undeterred, you press on. The group is standing in silence. You ask Richard, standing jauntily at one end, to talk about why he is standing where he is. Unsure what tone to adopt, he falls into a mock bravado. In the midst of Richard's comment, Jason, at the other end of the continuum, makes a taunting remark. There are titters up and down the line. Side conversations sprout here and there. You try to restore order: "It's important that we listen to one another." You are largely ignored. Other opinion leaders speak up, interrupting one another. There are now multiple speakers up and down the line, with others whispering conspiratorily. Most stand in silenced observation. Lamar, always quiet and thoughtful, looks at you as if to ask rhetorically, "*What* were you thinking?"

What *do* we think of this sad demise of a promising classroom activity? Is it too advanced for these students? Is it developmentally inappropriate? Is it too "touchy-feely"? Is it just random opinion stating, void of "rigor" and "content?" Whichever one of these standard analyses we choose, we will miss the deeper dynamic at work in this and other classroom encounters where students are presented with opportunities for authentic learning. Sadly, our students have learned well the lessons of the larger system. They have nearly forgotten how to learn. The blunt force of the manufacturing metaphor lands finally and with greatest impact on the tender psyches of children. Children, unlike raw material headed for the assembly line, are not inert matter, but mostly, in classrooms, teachers talk—in the interest of fixing content to children's minds. Student expression is often limited to the recitation of whatever fact or rudimentary concept is to be affixed in order to demonstrate that, indeed, it is affixed (even if only wobbily so and destined to fall off as soon as the test is passed). Of course, there are exceptions in every school and, for at least moments, in many classrooms, but the norm continues to be what, for over a century, an industrial mental model has led us to believe is the essential meaning of education. Our students adjust to this norm by denying on a daily basis their own interests, questions, and eagerness to engage with their age mates. We shush them into a state of deep alienation from their natural orientation to learning and socializing.

Given all of this, why is it any surprise to us that when we call on our students to ask questions and engage with their peers about important issues, to listen, to adjust their thinking, they don't know how. Such behavior, squashed in formal exercises, finds expression mostly through behavior that is secret and subversive of the official classroom norms: no talking, no copying, do your own work, follow directions, remain in your seat. When, occasionally, we organize our classrooms to nurture the natural learning inclinations of children, we get chaos, of course, because no one has coached them in how to do serious intellectual work in groups. Seeing the chaos, we conclude wrongly, "give them an inch and they'll take a mile." So we clamp down all the more, deepening their alienation from learning.

As thoughtful educators we need to acknowledge this history and the dynamics it has set in motion, in order to, first, counter the standard analyses for failed experiments with authentic learning, and, second, to begin to equip our students with the habits and capacities to re-embrace their desire to learn. We need to remember that when we design curriculum and classroom activities that call for real learning, our students will need significant coaching to help them remember what learning is and how to do it with their peers. In the aforementioned classroom encounter, when the proverbial "you" walked into the classroom to begin the continuum exercise, you forgot—against all logic—that your students were *not* accustomed to listening to one another as part of their work, that they had *not* been taught to express original ideas and were *not* expected by their teacher and classmates to do so, that they had *not* been made to feel safe in a context of intellectual give and take. Those are the skills we must coach them to develop and the beliefs we must persuade them are trustworthy. It takes time and requires a careful scaffolding of activities to develop. The key directive we need to remember is that while students have a powerful orientation toward learning, we should not assume that they possess the skills or experience to channel their creative energies. Those are skills that we, as more experienced persons, can teach them. If we are going to ask our students to do work that requires such skills, then we need to check what's already in place and what's not.

Teacher Talk

"I've worked here for many years, and I believe we turn out a solid product here at the Green River School." Larry Patterson, a veteran teacher and beloved wrestling coach, is holding forth in the faculty room during lunch. You are seated with several colleagues at Larry's table, where heads bob in silent approval of Larry's summary statement. You know that at least two others at the table are wincing inwardly at the analysis implied by Larry's remark. Larry is a believer in "the basics"—basic math skills, good grammar, orderly, five-paragraph essays, and an ample dose of content in history and science—an uncomplicated and a serviceable formula in his mind. But you and your silent colleagues know that Larry's notion of basics is misguided. How do you tease it apart? How do you offer something different? How do you engage Larry?

The dominant culture of schooling, in particular, the omnipresence of the manufacturing metaphor, is perpetuated most powerfully through the routine interactions of educators with each other. To the extent that we fail to challenge it when confronted, we ensure its continuation. But challenging the industrial mental model in the midst of our routine interactions carries risks. You could say, "I'm sorry, Larry, but I don't think of my students as products." You *could*, but in so doing you would likely create a condition of permanent discomfort, since Larry is there every time you enter the faculty room. He also teaches just two doors down the hall and is your daily neighbor on the first floor of B wing. Also, there are many on the faculty who share Larry's viewpoint, not just the "old-guard," but also younger teachers. Larry is a powerful presence in faculty meetings and well regarded in the community. You anger Larry at your peril. But ignore Larry and school will continue to reflect the ill-fitting, mechanistic metaphor that has dominated educational practice since Francis Parker's day. What to do?

Rob Evans, psychologist, educational consultant, author, and former teacher, speaks to this issue with deep understanding of the interpersonal challenges involved in changing a culture. There is a *human side* to school change, as the title of one of his books reminds us.[25] Evans suggests that people and systems are conservative by nature, mainly because change involves risk and discomfort. Therefore, someone who wishes to initiate change must establish that there is risk and discomfort associated with *not* changing, indeed, greater risk and greater discomfort. Change must be viewed as the preferred path, the path of less risk and less discomfort than maintaining the status quo, and not just by persons who are advocating for change but by others in the system who must implement the change. This sounds like a threat. It is not. It is quite the contrary, a warning that a train is coming, and folks had better get off the tracks. Once people recognize the danger, the next step is to begin to think about alternative courses of action. By taking this approach, organizations and the people in them begin to "unfreeze."[26]

So what are the risks associated with not changing? What are the risks associated with continuing to live inside the manufacturing metaphor and to imagine our work and our schools as a mechanistic system of production? What are the risks of Larry Patterson's view of schooling? Richard Murnane, professor at the Harvard Graduate School of Education, has studied the skills that are necessary in the new economy. He concludes that the traditional "basics" of reading, writing, and arithmetic are insufficient to equip high school graduates with what they will need for most middle-class jobs. Our economy has changed. Murnane's research shows that the number of blue-collar jobs, work that traditionally requires an ability to follow directions and to learn simple "basic" skills, has declined sharply since 1969—from 38 percent of employed adults to just under 25 percent.[27] Meanwhile, jobs that require higher-level thinking skills (managers, administrators, professional occupations, and technicians) are on the rise. Murnane concludes, "The three Rs are not less important, but they need to be tools for knowledge acquisition and communication. Expert thinking and complex communication are not new subjects to add to the curriculum. They should be at the center of instruction in every one of the existing subjects."[28]

In our terms, what Murnane has identified here are the consequences of the manufacturing metaphor, which has done a good job of preparing graduates to follow directions, read a training manual, and do fractions and decimals—Larry Patterson's view of school—but not to think beyond. Murnane's analysis requires us to imagine some very different metaphors if we are to help our students succeed as adults. But we don't want to alienate Larry Patterson because, as a career educator, Larry is not likely to leave, and if change is going to come to our schools, then Larry Patterson is going to need to be part of it. We want to win his partnership in the work that lies ahead. We must disabuse him of a view that is at best out of date. We must engage with him about the meaning of a public education at the dawning of the new millennium.

Public Engagement

"I'm looking at flat test scores. How do we get those up? You're the educator. You tell me," says Marissa May, parent and vocal citizen. As the superintendent of schools pondering how you will respond to a caustic question from a member of the public at a Board of Education meeting, you face a dilemma with well more than the usual two "horns." This particular beast has at least five. The first is that learning is reduced in this comment/question to test scores.

We know learning is more than that. The second is that talking about learning solely in terms of test scores—a la manufacturing metaphor—narrows the focus of education, and the extent to which we persist with that narrowed focus leads to a narrowed learning experience for our students and the sort of deep alienation apparent in the continuum exercise described earlier. The third is that the education establishment, as represented by state and federal departments of education and commercial publishers, endorses and promotes the reductivist analysis implied by the speaker's remark. Test scores have become the coin of the realm, minted in government offices and widely in circulation throughout the publishing industry. A comment that might in more reasonable times be dismissed as a crackpot idea suddenly reflects official state and federal policy! A fourth horn of this beastly dilemma is that test scores are viewed within the frame of this remark as an end in themselves. The question is not, how do we improve the learning that is measured by these tests, but how do we improve the test scores. Though these may seem like the same question, they are not, in terms of their practical consequences. If our goal is to improve test scores, then we will engage in a host of test-prep activities, the goal of which is to squeeze maximum test performance out of test takers. If our goal is to improve the learning measured by the tests, then we will redesign instruction to better meet stated objectives. A fifth horn sprouting from the remark is the apparent lack of agency by the person offering it. This problem is *yours*, Dr. Superintendent! In the world of education as industrial process, such an attitude is no surprise. What would any layperson know about the manufacturing process that goes on behind those brick walls?

So how *does* one answer this remark? To just answer it, of course, means to become complicit in its troubling analysis, but to challenge it in the moment presents hazards not dissimilar to the ones we face in challenging Larry Patterson's remark. In the moment, it is probably best to follow common sense by acknowledging Ms. May's concerns and reassuring her that you share those concerns and that you are doing everything you can to address them. However, the greater challenge lies in addressing the worldview that stands behind the remark. This is where we, as educators, must recognize that our work is not just about educating children, it is about educating the public and, more than that, it is about advocating for a thoughtful commitment to education within our schools and communities. No small task, as it runs counter to culturally embedded beliefs and dominant public policies.

Countering the Culture

What are some practical and effective ways to engage with the Larry Pattersons and Marissa Mays of our schools and communities?

1. Most of the time, people have good intentions, and most of the time it is fitting to affirm those intentions, to show solidarity in our common cause of student learning. (For those times when a person does not have good intentions, a different approach is probably warranted, but that is a different subject!)

2. In our own talk and our own actions, we need to demonstrate our commitment to thoughtful educational practices. We need to avoid manufacturing language and adopt language that better represents the complexity of learning and respect for students and adults engaged in it. Personally, I have found that language associated with child rearing and ecology provides a more appropriate metaphorical framework for education than the language of manufacturing. We nurture the growth of children. We till the soil and tend the seedlings. We cannot *make* them grow, but we can create conditions that are conducive to growth. They will not grow at the same rate or in the same ways. We celebrate the different ways in which they grow and express their beauty. The language we choose to employ is not a trivial matter. Linguist George Lakoff argues persuasively that, in fact, the metaphors we use to frame phenomena profoundly shape our thinking. He writes, ". . . the way we think, what we experience, and what we do every day is very much a matter of metaphor."[29] Though Lakoff has most recently gained public attention for his writing about language "framing" in the world of politics, the idea is applicable to education as well. The way we frame the discussion determines its outcome. We as educators need to reframe the debate just like politicians in order to make room for new and constructive possibilities.

3. We need to be active, not simply reactive, in our efforts to redirect education in more constructive ways. Responding to Larry Patterson or Marissa May in the moment is not a good way to educate the public. It only shames those we need as allies. Rather, we should design activities into the agendas of our meetings, the purpose of which is to advocate on behalf of thoughtful school practice and to make the case through evidence, demonstration, and expertise, as well as to cast the discussion with language that promotes a more thoughtful and respectful understanding of the nature of learning.

Case Closed

It is encouraging to observe that even with Parker's departure from the Quincy schools in 1880, there seems to have been a certain resiliency to the Quincy schools' humane approach to schooling. Two successive superintendents retain in their annual reports the language, at least, of thoughtful schools. One, for example, writes in his 1884 report, "It has been shown that a school in which the utmost uniformity of position is to be seen, and deathlike stillness prevails, may not be a well-governed school. The constant aim has been to give pupils such a degree of self-control as would enable them to govern themselves."[30] No doubt, the continuing presence of at least one Adams on the Quincy School Committee as late as 1882, as well as the family's omnipresence in community affairs, played a significant role in the endurance of Quincy's humane and thoughtful approach to schooling.

Today, the industrial mentality is more deeply embedded in the culture, even as the means of production in the United States are shifting in significant ways away from the centralized, product assembly, mass-production mode of the industrial era. The citizens of Quincy, though caught up in the industrial order in the 1870s, were still but a generation or two removed from an agrarian society, and the cultural imprint of the industrial world had not fully blunted their imagination. Today, the industrial system serves as *the* dominant metaphor for social organization. Thoughtful school people who advocate for humane schools must fight a deeply embedded popular conceptualization of schooling that includes not only industrial thinking but the "successful" application of industrial thinking to schools going back now several generations. For the vast majority of Americans today, it is hard to imagine something else. Nonetheless, the factors that promoted Quincy's success have relevance today. A related observation: as the industrial era fades, eventually, inevitably, so too will the power of its metaphors for social organization. What will replace them? Already, the language and thinking of the information age are permeating our social institutions. The information age *zeitgeist* offers the potential of both greater connectivity and depersonalization. As educators, we must proceed with an awareness of both the possibilities and perils of emerging technologies and the metaphorical power they will assert over social institutions.

Just as the Adams family provided money and respectability for Parker, so philanthropic organizations today can leverage the impact of humane and thoughtful school causes. Such national efforts as the Coalition of Essential Schools and the Annenberg Institute for School Reform have benefited from the largess of private foundations.

Thoughtful and imaginative school leaders, too, remain essential to the promotion of thoughtful school practice. Examples such as Ernest Boyer, John Goodlad, Theodore Sizer, and Deborah Meier have succeeded in effecting large-scale change through a combination of wisdom, charm, political savvy, and a deep personal commitment to the lives of children. At the school level, faculty self-selection continues to be a noted condition for effective learning communities. Also, various approaches to reducing class size and/or student load are repeatedly cited as significant forces behind improved learning.

Perhaps the most important understanding to take from the impressive accomplishments of the Quincy schools so long ago is to heed Francis Parker's warning that we not view the work there as a method or a system but as the natural consequence of thoughtful and humane reflection by those adults most closely involved in that institution where childhood and formal education intersect. Indeed, the Report of the Quincy School Committee for 1881 summarizes well Parker's legacy in its commentary on Parker's impact on the schools over the five years he served as superintendent. "He found them machines, he left them living organisms."[31]

2

The Fear Factor

Framing the Issue

It being one chief project of that old deluder, Satan, to keepe men from the knowledge of the scriptures, as in former time. . . . It is therefore ordered . . . [that] after the Lord hath increased [the settlement] to the number of fifty howshoulders, [they] shall forthwith appoint one within their town, to teach all such children as shall resorte to him, to write and read.[1]

Massachusetts Education Law of 1647
Enacted by the Colonial Legislature of
The Massachusetts Bay Colony

The genesis of American public education is a fear response. What motivated legislators in Massachusetts Bay Colony to pass the original enabling legislation for local schooling in 1647, the heart of which appears above, was fear of Satan. The Puritan culture of the era saw Satan and his minions as a very real, sometimes physically manifested, force in peoples' lives. Children, not yet fully chastened by the harsh behavioral codes of the time, were seen as particularly vulnerable to Satan's lures. Something had to be done. The reading of and adherence to a particular interpretation of Scripture was the chief means available to people to hold Satan at bay. Thus the teaching of reading to the young, mainly for the purpose of reading Scripture, was a crucial priority.

Fear has remained an influential force in public schooling in the United States. Throughout the history of slavery, fear of the people held in bondage drove whites to forcibly deny slaves access to the tools of literacy. To the waves of European immigrants in northern cities throughout the nineteenth century, educators and policy makers chose to respond out of fear by erecting a system that smothered all cultures of origin with a curriculum of "Americanization." Fear of communism drove a curriculum and school practices that extolled

31

capitalism and America's leadership role in the world while infusing science education with federal money to enhance the nation's technological prowess. Fear of violent factions opposed to America's global dominance has led to a curriculum infused with notions of foreign terrorists challenging democracy and freedom. And fear of high-stakes tests drives school leaders impulsively to ill-advised decisions about curriculum and instruction.

Fear is a psychological given. Social projects that fail to acknowledge or seek to eradicate fear are bound to fail. At the same time, enterprises that are driven predominantly by fear distort human relations. Rather than seeking to eradicate fear, we will be far more successful in pursuing our goals as educators if we seek to understand fear and channel it constructively. We need also to recognize that fear is a part of all of us. Fear can underlie the community's perception as it reacts to a school board decision. Fear can drive a principal concerned about out-of-control student behavior in her school. Fear may explain the reluctance of students to engage in imaginative work in their classes. Or, it may be the reason teachers fail to speak frankly when the superintendent asks for "honest feedback." How do we come to understand fear? How do we assess its distribution among the players in the realm of our work as educators? How do we constructively address fear in order to advance the work of schools?

Though psychology offers a great deal of insight into the power of and constructive responses to fear, this work does not pretend to offer a psychological analysis. History, however, can be instructive about the role fear has played and continues to play in schools, and the ways in which we as educators may constructively address its many manifestations in our work.

The case that follows offers an extended illustration of an instance of a community that became afraid, an imaginative and a gifted educator who failed to factor community fear into his efforts to nurture a very promising school, and, consequently, the tragic loss of a stunning opportunity for transformative change in educational practice. It is an instructive tragedy as relevant today as it was in 1837. From the telling of this story, we can gain insight into the role that fear plays in our professional lives and clues as to how we may respond appropriately.

Case in Point

In Boston in 1834, the machinery of cultural control was shifting gears. The powerful grip once exerted by Calvinism and original sin was loosening, while the formidable gears of industrialism and urban bureaucracy were only just being forged. Industrial manufacture was a new idea. The crucial impact that manufacturing as metaphor for social organization was to have on society as a whole and schooling in particular in succeeding generations was a small wave slowly gathering heft and height far offshore.

Here was a place and a time when thoughtful school practice might shoot up through temporarily loosened soil, between the hard frost of Calvinist fear and the paving over of industrialization. It did so in the romantic philosophical movement known as transcendentalism. Bronson Alcott, one of the leaders of the transcendentalist movement, founded a tuition-based primary school in 1834, known as the Temple School, attended by the children of Boston's elite families. The school was based on Alcott's deep belief in the genius of children and dedicated to the liberation of their imagination.

What is most notable about Alcott's school is not so much its thoughtful philosophy as its spectacular demise. Within three short years, the Temple School, and Alcott with it, went from toast-of-the-town to leper outcast. The forces that bring a thoughtful school into existence as well as those that bring it down—hard—are plain to see in the story of the Temple School. In this case, those forces had mainly to do with community fear.

To understand the cultural context in which the Temple School emerged, and the culturally rooted fears that engulfed it, we need to first understand the main religious beliefs and religious institutions of the day. For almost two centuries, the idea of original sin, so important to New England's Congregational churches, held Boston in a tight cultural grip. But in the early decades of the nineteenth century, this ideological hold on New England institutions—including family, church, and school—declined considerably. The decline was brought on by a splintering within the Church, the arrival of immigrant Catholics from Europe, and the rise of secular interpretations of child development.

In the later decades of the eighteenth century, some Congregationalist ministers began to openly question basic Church beliefs such as original sin, that is, the idea that people, without God's intervention, are essentially bad. This led to the breakup of many churches. Because the Congregational Church of that time was a loose network of mainly independent congregations, there was no church hierarchy to enforce one view or the other, and because a more optimistic view of the individual than that allowed by Calvinism was gaining popularity among New Englanders, many congregations split. Protestors would leave and form their own "liberal" Congregational church nearby. Even today, on opposite sides of many a New England town common, one may find a Congregational and a Unitarian church, legacy to this eighteenth-century schism.

The Liberal movement spread shortly to Harvard College, where Liberals took control in the first decade of the 1800s. Church historians have estimated that by the end of the protest movement, around 1840, all but one of Boston's churches had been won over by the Liberal movement.[2] Spokespersons for conservative beliefs acknowledged this transformation in angry declarations.

Harriet Beecher Stowe, writing of her father who was the chief spokesperson for traditional church beliefs and who moved to Boston in the contentious days of 1826, reports,

> When Dr. Beecher came to Boston, Calvinism or orthodoxy was the despised and persecuted form of faith. It was the dethroned royal family wandering like a permitted mendicant in the city where once it had held court, and Unitarianism reigned in its stead.[3]

The Church's power was further diluted by the growing presence of Roman Catholics, whose ranks swelled from 2,000 in 1820 to over 20,000 by 1835.[4] These numbers would soon explode with the massive Irish emigration at mid-century, but even in these early decades, Roman Catholicism was becoming a force.

At the same time, a secular counterpart to religious liberalism was also making its way into the heart of New England culture. Childhood was being thought of in very different, and more positive, terms. Historians of the era point to the appearance between the 1820s and 1860 of popular magazines and books focusing on children and child development.[5]

Driving these changes in New England was the growing popularity of English philosopher John Locke's view of the human mind as a tabula rasa, or blank slate. If an infant's mind was truly a tabula rasa, then the infant could not be inherently bad or good—only blank. The possibilities for human learning were wide open. There was a shift in the popular view of the individual from idleness, frailty, weakness, and fear to hope, possibility, and the potential for good. Consequently, schooling became the means not just of keeping idle hands busy but the engine of human possibility in a civic culture. Horace Mann, chief school leader of the day, reflected this shift when he declared, "Men are cast-iron; but children are wax. Strength expended upon the latter may be effectual, which would make no impression upon the former."[6] The timing was right for someone like Bronson Alcott to step onto the Boston scene.

Amos Bronson Alcott is best known as one of the founders and main spokespersons of the transcendentalist school of thought. He is the father of Louisa May Alcott, author of *Little Women*. He is also the founder of Fruitlands, an ill-fated utopian experiment plowed from the hills west of Boston, and the inspiration for Louisa May's book. Prior to these notable contributions to American culture, however, Bronson Alcott worked as a schoolmaster who, at mid-career, founded a short-lived school in Boston in 1834. It closed just three years later.

Alcott was born in rural Connecticut in 1799. His early education was in a rural schoolhouse typical of the era, which meant that attendance was irregular, teachers came and went, and the building was damp and cold in winter. Though his parents were poorly schooled farmers, his uncle was Yale educated and served as principal of the Cheshire Academy.

After completing school and working several years as a peddler of manufactured goods in the rural South, Alcott decided to try his hand as schoolmaster in his own Connecticut environs. Over several years, he developed a controversial reputation as a teacher who encouraged his pupils to use their own minds—a not entirely welcome habit in communities accustomed to simple instruction in the three R's, enforced with a heavy dose of physical discipline. Quite contrary to the fear-driven Calvinistic influences on education by which he was surrounded, Alcott grew to admire the innocence and intelligence of the children he taught.

Alcott began to gain notoriety. As far away as Boston, a writer for the *Boston Recorder and Telegraph* described Alcott's school in Cheshire as "the best common school in the State, perhaps in the United States."[7] This praise, however, only incited the Calvinist faithful, who were already wary of Alcott's ways with their children. An alternative school—ironically, more traditional in philosophy—shortly sprang up in Cheshire, and Alcott closed his own school and returned home. Similar controversy followed him in Bristol, where he served as schoolmaster for a year. Deeply frustrated, he decided to quit Connecticut and its Calvinist ways permanently for Boston.

Once in Boston, Alcott immersed himself in the intellectual life of the city, chiefly by attending the Unitarian churches. Shortly, he was invited to open an infant school. His biographer, Odell Shepard, reports:

> He taught his children as individuals, recognizing in each of them a separate soul with which it was his privilege—that is, if he could be patient and kind and skillful enough—to come into an affectionate parental relation.[8]

In no time, Alcott had fans among his pupils' parents, the clergy, and the press. Boston seemed to embrace Alcott as the modern antidote to Calvinist fear. In rapid succession, he became superintendent of a Sunday school and, in the autumn of 1828, he started an elementary school for boys, which also was heralded instantly as a success. He also married Abigail May, the sister of a clergyman friend, whose acquaintance he had made some years earlier in Connecticut.

Alcott's fame in Boston grew, in the midst of which an invitation came from a wealthy Philadelphian Quaker visitor to open a school there. Alcott, seeking something of a sabbatical from the intensity of his Boston work, accepted. This was indeed a period (some four years in length) of less demanding work and less public attention during which he read voraciously. But his home was Boston, and it was there, through the preliminary work of his friends, William

Ellery Channing and Elizabeth Peabody, that thirty pupils were procured for a school that Alcott would lead. He returned with his wife and new daughters, rooms were obtained in the Masonic Temple on Tremont Street, and the school came to be known (taking full advantage of the opportunity for a grand title) as the Temple School.

The most detailed, if also most deeply partisan, source of information about the Temple School comes from a book authored by Alcott's assistant, Elizabeth Peabody, and published in December 1836. Ironically, the book also precipitated the school's rapid demise. The Temple School closed for lack of pupils within months of the book's publication.

Record of Mr. Alcott's School Exemplifying the Principles and Methods of Moral Culture [9] is attributed to A. Bronson Alcott with a simple acknowledgment that Elizabeth Peabody served as "recorder." Consisting largely of classroom observations referring to Alcott in the third person, the narrative suggests that true authorship was Peabody's. I will therefore refer to Peabody as author.

A number of pages early in the text are devoted to a description of the opulent physical condition of the school. An engraved portrait of the school's interior also appears on one page. Busts of philosophers are complemented by Gothic architectural elements, colored carpets, and bright, large windows.

On the first day of school, according to Peabody's account, there were twenty students: seventeen boys under age ten and three older girls. "Mr. Alcott sat behind his desk, and the children were placed in chairs in a large arc around him; the chairs so far apart that they could not easily touch each other. He then asked each one separately what idea he or she had of the purpose of coming to school." A dialogue ensues eliciting a range of issues, topics, and thoughts from the students. The account continues. "Simple as all this seems, it would hardly be believed what an evident exercise it was to the children, to be led of themselves to form and express these conceptions and few steps of reasoning. Every face was eager and interested."[10]

Socratic dialogue became a common feature of life at the Temple School, together with extended silent periods for students to write in their journals. As the school year got under way Alcott established a routine of journaling for one hour at the beginning of each day. Peabody reports:

> December 30th.—When I came to school, I found all the children in their seats, at their lessons. Mr. Alcott, who was walking round as usual, was saying to one of the journalists: You are engaged in recording what happens out of you; its advantage is to make you feel and remember what effect all outward events, and your action on what is outward, may have on your inward state of mind. You write down the picture made by your mind on things. I hope you will soon write the thoughts and feelings that come up from your

soul about these things. These thoughts and feelings are your inward life. Do you understand what I mean by this assertion,—the spiritual world is the inward life of all things?[11]

The overarching purpose of journaling was to plumb the depths of the soul. Alcott was working from a mind-set suggested to him early on by his contact with the Quakers and their notion of "inner light," then furthered by his readings of the English romantics. Peabody writes, "Imagination is the soul's shaping power. . . . We need schools not alone for the inculcation of knowledge, but for the development of Genius—the creative attribute of spirit."[12]

Even the physical layout of the room encouraged this tendency toward individual introspection. "The desks for the scholars, with conveniences for placing all their books in sight, and with black tablets hung over them, which swing forward when they wish to use them, are placed against the wall round the room, that when in their seats for study no scholar need look at another."[13]

Alcott seems to have been a gentle and positive presence in the room, simultaneously encouraging his pupils and insisting on order and decorum. The students' early efforts at writing, though often illegible, were encouragingly received by Alcott:

> . . . as they exhibited their strange copies, [he] betrayed no misgivings as to the want of resemblance; nor did Mr. Alcott rudely point it out. He took the writing for what it was meant to be; knowing that practice would at once mend the eye and hand, but that criticism would check the desirable courage and self-confidence.[14]

Alcott's approach to writing instruction was more than a clever tactic; rather, it was an expression of his deeply held convictions that education was a drawing out of the child, an "unveiling of the soul." Peabody notes, "There is no greater illusion than the common idea of the method of learning to read by pronouncing pages of matter, which is not moving the heart and mind of the reader."[15]

Alcott's beliefs were also reflected in his approach to classroom discipline.

> . . . Mr. Alcott is so thoroughly convinced that all effectual government must be self-government, that he much prefers that all the operations of school should obviously stand still than that they should apparently go on while really standing still or going back in any individual instance. If it should be objected to this principle, that the good are here made to wait upon the bad, it may be answered, that the good are learning the divinest part of

human action, when they are taught to wait upon the bad for their improvement.[16]

Several pages later, Peabody's account reveals that Alcott experimented with a form of punishment whereby the guilty student would be required to administer a stroke on the teacher's hand:

> On the morning this was announced . . . there was a profound stillness. Boys who had never been affected before, and to whom bodily punishment was a very small affair, as far as its pain was concerned, were completely sobered.[17]

Alcott stood at the cusp of an educational revolution. His sympathetic manner, inquiry-based curriculum, and emphasis on individual reflection stood on its head the mind-numbing, fear-driven approach to schooling and promised to nurture thoughtful, independent-minded pupils. Unfortunately, it was not to last, as Alcott's radical departure from well-worn traditions, coupled with his failure to address growing public fears, led to the school's rapid demise. Though Boston was proudly Unitarian in manner and speech, the deep imprint of Calvinist culture lay just under the surface.

At its peak, enrollment in the Temple School rose to forty students. Visitors shortly began to arrive, and soon Alcott was earning positive recognition for his work with children. All appeared to be well. But, as it turned out, Mr. Alcott's outspoken views proved too liberal even for Unitarian Boston.

Perhaps the first hint of problems came in the words of the influential Boston preacher, William Ellery Channing. Initially, Channing had given his blessing to the school, but he gradually grew concerned with the level of introspection encouraged among the children. He wrote in a letter to Peabody, "I want light as to the degree to which the mind of the child should be turned inward. The free development of the spiritual nature may be impeded by too much analysis of it."[18] Channing's influence in Boston was enormous, and to the extent that he may have shared this same view publicly, he would be sowing seeds of discomfort with Alcott's work.

Alcott's unorthodox thinking also became more widely known through his practice of entertaining public "Conversations." This was the age of the public lecture, and lecture halls known as lyceums were springing up all over to accommodate itinerant speakers who provided culture and entertainment. Alcott launched his own speaking series, but rather than delivering in a presentational format, he conducted his Conversations as Socratic dialogues with his audience, just as was his teaching style at the Temple School.

In November 1836, he began a series of Conversations on Friday nights at his school, open to the public, on the life of Christ. In the course of this series he made clear that he viewed Christ as a very spiritual man but not divine, and that he viewed Christianity as a fine religion but just one among several fine religions. These views, though not unheard of in Unitarian Boston, were nevertheless controversial. The previous fall, Alcott had engaged in a similar round of conversations with his students at school. As Mr. Alcott's views became known, and as the intimation spread that he was advancing his views with his pupils, both parents and the wider public began to entertain serious doubts about this Connecticut schoolteacher they had so warmly welcomed into Boston society. During what Shepard aptly calls the "whispering campaign" of 1836, enrollment fell from forty to twenty-five by the fall of 1836.[19] The whispering may well have also been about a simple and veiled reference to sexuality in his Conversations, published later that year as part of his *Conversations on the Gospels,* where, in response to a student question, he states:

> . . . The physiological facts, sometimes referred to, are only a sign of the spiritual assistance of the atmosphere. This is the birth of the rose. It typifies the bringing forth of the spirit by pain and labor and patience. . . . And a mother suffers when she has a child. When she is going to have a child she gives up her body to God, and He works upon it in a mysterious way and, with her aid, brings forth the child's Spirit in a little Body of its own; and when it has come she is blissful.[20]

Though quaint by contemporary standards, this oblique reference was nothing short of scandalous to proper Bostonians.

Elizabeth Peabody had become sufficiently alarmed to leave the school in the summer of 1836. Having already penned her *Record,* and knowing of Alcott's intention to publish a further volume based on notes taken by her and others, she wrote an awkward letter to him seeking some way to distance herself from the manuscript. "I feel more and more that these questionable parts ought not to go into the printed book, at least that they must be entirely disconnected with me." Later in the same letter, she writes, ". . . I must desire you to put a preface of your own before mine, and express in it, in so many words, that on you rests all the responsibility of introducing the subjects, and that your Recorder did not entirely sympathize or agree with you with respect to the course taken. . . ."[21] The level of anxiety demonstrated by Peabody is evidence that gossip about Alcott's inappropriate views was already afoot. Alcott's response to Peabody's various pleas was to take passages that he thought might offend Peabody's sensibilities and consign them to footnotes and an appendix at the end of the book. The result of this act, however, was simply to highlight for the reading public all of the juiciest elements of the book.

The most significant event in the fall of Bronson Alcott and the Temple School was the publication of his *Conversations on the Gospels* in early 1837.

Reaction in the Boston press was almost immediate. A piece in the *Boston Courier* signed by "A Parent," ran as follows:

> We cannot repress our indignation at the love of notoriety, for it can be nothing else, which will lead a man to scorn the truth and the best interest of society—and boldly decrying public opinion and the sentiments of the wise and good, to pollute the moral atmosphere throw a stumbling block in the path of improvement, and say to the travelers therein "Thus far shalt thou go, and no further!" . . . It were a venial error in Mr. Alcott had he simply published the crude remarks of his pupils, but he has gone further. He seemed to delight in his own person in directing their attention to the more improper subjects—and when they appeared with intuitive perception to shrink from contact with them, he has forced their minds to grapple with them. . . . Mr. Alcott should hide his head in shame.[22]

The editor of the same paper wrote:

> *The Conversations on the Gospels* is a more indecent and obscene book (we say nothing of its absurdity) than any other we ever saw exposed for sale on a bookseller's counter. Mr. A. interrogates his pupils on subjects which are universally excluded from promiscuous companies of men and women.[23]

"Venial," "crude," "improper," "indecent," and "obscene." The newspapers continued on in this vein. Meanwhile, the public outcry became so great that mob violence threatened. In his journal for "April, Week XV," Alcott writes, "At one time the excitement threatened a mob. The plan was to make the assault at one of my Friday evening Conversations, but no such outrage attempted, and the minds of the disaffected are now settling into quietude."[24] A note he penned to a parent, dated February 18, 1837, asks whether an increase in tuition from fifteen dollars a quarter to twenty-five dollars would be acceptable.[25] Though the letter makes no mention of it, surely the increase in tuition was needed to offset declining enrollments. During the spring of 1837, enrollment decreased to ten, and the school moved to the basement of the Masonic Temple.[26]

Alcott wrote to his friend Emerson in May:

> I opened school on Monday with 10 pupils. These are all I fancy that this good and wise city intend to lend me during this quarter. So I have made up my mind to walk to and fro, and do for these whatsoever I may, waiting for light as this may be vouchsafed. Bread comes quite as easily and with less anxiety in this way as in any

other. And so for the present I shall continue to teach. Possibly at some day, I may take the benefit of your suggestion, and turn this matter over to other hands.[27]

By September, only four pupils remained, and in June 1838, with just three pupils remaining, Alcott closed the school. Even the Unitarian clergy turned against him, as his friend George Ripley informed him that they regarded him as "an interloper into the theological field."[28]

Larger Lessons

Bronson Alcott failed to consider the force of fear in the running of his school. He underestimated the conservative currents beneath the liberal surface of Boston culture. And when community anxiety surfaced, he failed in any way to address it. Oftentimes, so do we. In both small and large ways, we somehow manage to not notice what to other observers would be obvious warning signals, until it is too late. Margaret Mead once commented, "If fish were anthropologists, the one thing they would fail to notice is the water."[29] Sometimes, we, too, are so immersed in our school reform schemes that we fail to take note of the ways in which fear—either in ourselves or others—is playing a counterproductive role, largely because it goes unnoticed.

In initiating a new writing or math program, for example, what ideological land mines—that may have little to do with the substance of the program—lay in wait? Which partisan group has the new program already on its watch list of heretical practices? What iconic elements of the traditional high school does it disrupt: testing, teacher-centered instruction, individualistic achievement, competition, patriotism? What existing programs does it threaten to substantially or symbolically diminish?

It matters not whether the substance of our innovation actually threatens what the public values; what matters is whether the public *perceives* it as a threat. According to Peabody's account, Alcott was scrupulous about allowing his students to draw their own conclusions to charged questions, but the public perception was that he was proselytizing in the classroom. In fact, Alcott's Socratic dialogues raised questions and allowed the pupil room to draw his or her own conclusions. Peabody's final chapter ("Explanatory") in her *Record of Mr. Alcott's School* persuasively shows this to be the case.

He does not wish the children to think that the meaning of Scripture is a matter of authority; and this is the chief reason why he does not decide in favor of particular views, dogmatically. He thinks it is enough to start the mind on some subject, to "wake the echo that will not sleep again," and lays out to guard them from error, rather by the general influences of his moral and intellectual discipline than by giving them the formulas of any creed. So successful has he proved to be, in avoiding controverted points, and keeping free from the technology of sect, that one day, when two ladies—one a Trinitarian, and the other a Humanitarian—were present at a lesson on the first chapter of John, each left the room, saying to Mr. Alcott, "I perceive that my views are taught here."[30]

Nonetheless, despite Alcott's apparent effort to not proselytize, public perception to the contrary is what mattered. Canadian scholar Michael Fullan has devoted a career to the problem of school change. He has studied a wide range of school sites to understand the dynamics of all sorts of school reform efforts. One common factor that he finds at work in many otherwise different circumstances is the failure of those leading a change effort to consider the *subjective* meaning of the change for those who will be at the receiving end of it. In a chapter from his *New Meaning of Educational Change*, he gets at the essence of this meaning with a reference to Peter Marris:

> When those who have power to manipulate changes act as if they have only to explain, and when their explanations are not at once accepted, shrug off opposition as ignorance or prejudice, they express a profound contempt for the meaning of lives other than their own. For the reformers have already assimilated these changes to their purposes, and worked out a reformulation which makes sense to them, perhaps through months or years of analysis and debate. If they deny others the chance to do the same, they treat them as puppets dangling by the threads of their own conceptions.[31]

Fear is a crucial part of the subjective meaning of change, particularly when change is *done to us* by someone else. When we, as initiators of change, ignore the potential and/or actual fears that our school reform actions or perceived actions may inspire in others, we seal the doom of our well-intended projects.

The locus of fear, as we have been discussing it so far, resides in others; it is the fear that others have of our efforts as school reformers, the fears that Bronson Alcott so brazenly ignored in Boston a century and a half ago. But the fear factor is sometimes rooted in the unexamined anxieties *we* feel within *ourselves*. Why do I not give honest feedback when asked? Why do I take a more cautious step than I would really prefer? Why do I lash out aggressively against certain individuals? What am I afraid of?

"What am I so afraid of?" is not just a rhetorical question. It is a question we ought to be in the habit of regularly asking ourselves in situations where we sense in ourselves either hesitation or perhaps too much readiness. When the impulse at the root of our behavior is fight or flight, it is good practice to pause before we act. We know from psychology that being able to name our fear is a crucial first step in constructively addressing it and incorporating it productively into our actions. Naming it gives us power over our fear and grants us just enough psychic distance from it to employ that trait that has made us as a species the success that we are: critical reason.

Classroom Encounter

Consider the following classroom encounter:

In response to growing concern that math instruction needs to more actively engage students, your math department is considering revamping prevailing practice. Typically, in your school, a math class begins with a review of problems assigned the previous day. Sometimes this involves students demonstrating work at the board, while other times it means you, the teacher, perched on your stool at the front of the room next to the overhead projector, eliciting input from members of the class. After the homework review is completed, the day's topic is introduced, explained, and demonstrated. Students are guided through a sample problem or two, and the assignment is given from the textbook. If there is time remaining in the period, students begin their homework with coaching from you.

Recently, a consultant to the district spent a week observing math classes, reviewing textbooks, and reviewing student work. The report, while lauding the mathematical knowledge and pedagogical skill of the teachers, confirmed that legions of students are, indeed, quite disengaged.

At this point in the unfolding of events, you, as one of the math teachers in question, begin to feel a tinge of anxiety. There's something wrong with my instruction? Who is this consultant to tell us what to do? If we know our subject and we're good teachers, as the consultant confirms, why do we need to change? You find yourself at the receiving end of someone else's change effort, even before any change is announced, because you sense it coming. After all, the assistant superintendent for curriculum and instruction, with the blessing of your department chair, hired the consultant, who saw a need, maybe a need to improve instruction, or maybe a need to make her or his mark as a school leader. Objectively, this effort may result in changes to curriculum planning, instructional practice, and assessment practice. Such changes are technical in nature. Subjectively, however, these events go much deeper than the technical level and are already causing all sorts of emotional disturbance among you and your teaching colleagues: fear of the unknown, diminishment of self-worth and efficacy, and maybe anger that your carefully orchestrated routines managing enormously complex work will be needlessly disrupted. All of these emotions are accompanied by an overwhelming need to make sense of an uncertain and emerging workplace reality. How does one protect what is valuable from capricious change? How does one remain open to beneficial change? How does one thoughtfully navigate this process? While there is no simple answer, because every situation is different and complex, some principles can guide your way when the fear of change threatens to overwhelm the merits of the change itself.

Principle 1: Avoid responding before examining the facts. There are plenty of stock responses that can be thrown at situations involving change that will provide an easy rationale for either opposition or support—as you wish. Here are some stock rationales handy for opposition:

1. We tried it before, and it didn't work.

2. That might work in School Two, but it won't work here in School One, because we're different.

3. There's nothing wrong with what we're doing; the real problem is
   permissive parents;
   television;
   video games; and
   MySpace.

4. This is just administrator Maria or administrator Bob polishing their resume.

5. This will be bad for kids.

6. It's a great idea in theory, but . . .

One or more of these stock rationales for opposition will hold some appeal for almost any situation.

Many stock rationales also exist for support. Here's a short list:

1. We need to do *something*.

2. This worked really well in School Two.

3. It's not all that big a change, and it will make a real difference.

4. Everybody's behind it.

5. This will be good for kids.

Like the opposition rationales, one or more of these will find appeal in most situations.

It is possible that in any given circumstance one of these rationales—either supportive or opposing—will actually fit the facts, but frequently we assert one of these rationales *before* examining the facts. We are overcome by fear of change, and thus we pick a convenient path that allows us to reject whatever change is being suggested, or to embrace whatever change appears attractive. If we assert one of these before really examining the facts, then we are allowing ourselves to be guided purely by our emotions, and in many cases involving change, the chief emotion will be fear. Many school decisions ultimately get decided on this basis. One of the chief barriers to thoughtful practice is action driven impulsively by fear.

Principle 2: Examine the facts and judge on the merits. This is a corollary to principle 1. If we can withhold judgment long enough to really look objectively at our circumstances, the proposed change, who benefits from the change, who "pays" for it, and what the cost is, literally and figuratively, then we will judge far more wisely.

When my oldest daughter was young, she took art lessons from a woman who lived nearby. My daughter's teacher explained to me once that what she teaches her students to do, often, is not about artistic technique. Rather, she said, what she teaches them is *to see*. She explained this to me again for the purpose of this text:

> Half of what I teach is art, the other half is how to see. Very often your brain tells you what it thinks it's seeing, rather than letting your eyes tell you what you're actually seeing. For example: if I say the word chair, you immediately picture a chair. That preknown image in your brain affects what you think you're seeing. Your brain knows that all four chair legs are the same size, but if you draw what you actually see, the legs will not be the same length. Your brain will tell you that you're drawing the legs different lengths is wrong because if you measure them—they're all equal; but you have to tell your brain to shut up and actually draw and trust what you see, or the chair will never look correct.[32]

This insight is useful for educators facing change. How often do we respond to what we imagine as opposed to what we see if we really open our eyes? When we do open our eyes, and we see the real circumstance before us, it usually reveals itself in more complex and ambiguous terms than any of our oversimplified, knee-jerk emotional responses. As we begin to develop a judgment about the real situation, it will likely be somewhat more tentative and nuanced. This may lead to complications with colleagues.

The math curriculum example we are dealing with here has to do with instructional practice, what we as educators do in the classroom. So far, we have been looking at this example as an aspect of classroom work. As we move into this next section, "Teacher Talk," we will continue this example and examine its ramifications for our interactions with our colleagues.

Teacher Talk

You stroll into the faculty room, the day after the math consultant's report has been announced. The energetic buzz that accompanied the announcement yesterday has mellowed into a mood of knowing confidence. Many have made up their minds. The speed with which this has happened makes you wonder whether people have examined the facts or whether emotion—fear—is leading the way. At one table you hear: "Administrator Maria is just polishing her resume." "Our demographics are completely different from School Two." "This can only be bad for kids." You stroll into the copy room adjacent to the faculty room. There, two of your colleagues are at the copy machine. In a quieter voice than what you heard next door, one person says, "We need to do *something*." And, "It's not that big a change really; and the payoff for kids is huge."
What do you do? It seems that everybody has already made up their minds! You wonder, are you slow, uninformed, naïve, plain old stupid? What meeting did you miss where apparently everybody discussed the issue? In all likelihood, you missed no meeting and you are no less informed than everyone else. You, however, are trying to see the chair, not what you imagine to be the chair.

There's nothing like solidarity to help strengthen personal belief. If others are saying what you yourself wish to believe, then you will likely believe it all the more, even if it has nothing to do with reality. How often in political dramas are statements made and repeated widely without anyone ever pausing to examine the facts? In Bronson Alcott's case, a mob threatened to attack his home. I would bet that no one in that mob had actually read Alcott's books or visited his school or spoken with him directly. This suggests another principle.

Principle 3: Insist that others examine the facts too. If you stop to "see the chair," but everyone around you is drawing what they imagine the chair to be, then you will have no impact on the outcome of the change, and you will likely grow cynical of your surroundings. If the weakest response to change is to go solely with your emotions—your fears—without examining the facts, then the next weakest response is to examine the facts and fail to do anything about it. A truly strong and thoughtful response requires that you insist that others examine the facts too. Be in the habit of asking both supporters and opponents, how do you know? "This improvement will increase test scores!" *How do you know?* Administrator Maria is just polishing her resume. *How do you know?* It's not that big of a change anyway? *How do you know?* Because the knee-jerk emotional response is so powerful, and because confirmation of one's response by others helps solidify belief, it is crucial that as you examine the facts, you also insist that those around you examine the facts as well. This may not build immediate popularity, but it will likely engender respect; moreover, it will increase the likelihood of a better educational outcome.

So far, we've been discussing the math example from the standpoint of teachers, at the receiving end of change. Sometimes the receiving end is where you happen to be. Other times, you are the initiator of change—whether teacher or administrator. Understanding and constructively addressing with one's colleagues the subjective meaning of change from the initiator's side of the equation is equally important. Remember Michael Fullan's (and Peter Marris's) admonition above: When initiators get to the point of launching a change, they have already worked through the subjective aspects of the change process themselves. They have fully incorporated it into their view of the workplace, their work, and their professional identity.[33]

The most important difference between the initiator of change and the implementer, who is just learning about it, is that one has moved through the emotional, subjective aspects of the change and the other has not. The subjective side is far more important than the objective substance of the change, since it is where final decisions tend to get made and judgments are formed. As Fullan points out, it is the height of arrogance and insensitivity for initiators of change to deny to others the emotional response that they themselves have experienced. Therefore, one important key to the successful initiation of change is to grant room for the emotional response to work itself out. This means allowing your colleagues to vent, but it goes beyond that. It means an openness to considering and responding substantively to the legitimate concerns they raise. To allow others room to thrash about emotionally without allowing the possibility that such thrashing may, in fact, be connected to legitimate concerns about the merits of the change idea is condescending. It means that you regard your colleagues' emotional response as nothing more than a tantrum that will pass, which you can then follow with a regimen of persuasion, followed by swift implementation. To suggest that initiation is simply about persuading others that your idea is good or obtaining "buy in" is to completely miss what it means to conduct thoughtful, collaborative work. In order for change to take hold and last, it must be rooted in the culture, in the beliefs and values of the organization. To accomplish this, the line between initiator and implementer must be erased. This suggests a fourth principle.

Principle 4: Thoughtful and lasting change begins with the right questions and *leads* to good ideas. It does not *begin* with ideas. Imagine you are the math department chair. The assistant superintendent has indicated that she has a strong sense that students are largely disengaged. She says you need to do something about it. Suppose that in beginning to address this concern you ask, with your math colleagues, what does student engagement look like? Suppose you follow this by designing a protocol for the consultant to examine student engagement in classrooms based on a rubric you construct with your colleagues. Suppose you then ask the consultant not to issue a report but simply to present that data from his classroom observations with all personal identifiers removed. Suppose you then use a simple protocol to examine the data with your math colleagues, asking the question, what is happening in the classroom when students are engaged? What should we, as teachers, continue to do, and what should we do differently in order to increase student engagement?

In this scenario, the line between initiator of change and implementer of change is blurred, because both are going through the process together, present with one another as both the subjective and objective aspects of the potential change unfold. The process begins with a question and ends with an idea or series of ideas that all have some connection to and quite likely some commitment to. As compelling and logical as this order of events is, it represents the reverse of the usual approach to school change, which begins with an idea and often sputters to a halt clogged with unanswered questions. Fear at the initiator's end of the change process is fear that one's ideas won't be realized. The best way to allay this fear is to begin instead with a question. Fear at the implementor's end of the change process is fear of loss of control. The best was to allay this fear is through authentic collaboration.

Public Engagement

Much of the dynamic at work around instructional practice and interaction with colleagues is the same with the community that extends beyond the school. Anyone who has ever attended a town meeting in New England or a city/town council elsewhere has likely witnessed stock responses of support or opposition rooted in emotion and void of any reference to fact and actual circumstance. People love to see the chair they imagine instead of the chair that is in front of them! After all, it is much easier. Present also in these settings is the groupthink that gets generated by the repetition of stock responses by others responding equally with emotion and equally without any examination of facts. Before long, if, as in Alcott's case, these fears go unattended, an angry mob is threatening to gather outside of your home! In like manner, ideas put forward by leaders in these settings often sputter to a halt, mired in questions that morph into comments and judgments as audience skepticism hardens like quick-drying cement to widespread opposition.

In the same way that we, as educational leaders, need to engage colleagues with questions and collaborative inquiry, we need to likewise engage our various publics. Board meetings are not the place to begin, since they are designed by the rigidity of parliamentary or other highly formalized procedures to promote opinion stating, position taking, debating, and the battle for votes. Better to engage our publics initially in informal settings where real questions may be raised, ideas tried out tentatively, uncertainties voiced, and ambiguity and complexity acknowledged collectively.

We will also do well to have our political antennae up, that is, to be attuned to the prejudices and biases of our communities. If there is a "Concerned Citizens for Fiscal Responsibility" group that has sprung up, then we need to anticipate how it will likely respond in discussions. This is not to say that we should prepare our arguments in advance—quite the opposite. It is to say that we need to try to understand the group's root concerns, acknowledge these concerns, and surface the competing concerns that must be reckoned with. Similarly, it means that we also need to inject real data into the public discussion, a feature so often missing!

In the math example, imagine that you are the assistant superintendent. A week after your initial discussion with the math department chairperson, the two of you check in with each other for a progress update. You learn that the math department is asking collectively what student engagement looks like and how it will deploy the consultant. Together, the two of you decide that parents and students could contribute as well to this process, and that including them in some appropriate way in the discussion will help achieve the same benefits of including the teachers. You agree to ask the PTA to identify a dozen or so parents whose children are enrolled in the full range of math courses in the high school who they might be willing to engage in a kind of focus group discussion about their children's experiences in math class. You invite them to an evening of math discussion. You also ask the school board to send a representative in order to be connected to the process. You decide as well to engage the principal, asking him if he could invite students to a lunchtime discussion of math at the high school to ask them—without identifying teachers or classroom specifics—to talk about the kinds of activities that they believe help them most in learning math. A high school principal in central Massachusetts engages in such a practice on a regular basis, not just on the topic of math but for all subjects.[34] In all of these conversations, you take good notes, which are shared with all parties to serve as the basis of further conversations—rooted in actual facts—and, together, you move toward ideas for improvement.

There are, of course, challenges involved in an approach such as this. It will be very easy for the math teachers to feel that they are being criticized, and it will therefore be important to highlight the ways in which their work is engaging students and to build on those practices. It will also be important to acknowledge the forces beyond classroom practice that teachers have little or no control over, such as class size, student demographics, state and federal mandates, and so forth, yet at the same time to hold the focus steadily on what lies *within* the power of the math department to accomplish.

By engaging all parties—teachers, administrators, parents, students, and board members—in conversation on appropriate questions centered on student learning, the fear factor can be substantially diminished, and student learning can be substantially enhanced. In the process, a collaborative culture will grow from the relationships forged in meetings and discussions. As trust is established, fear will diminish.

Countering the Culture

Fear finds its roots in the perception of loss of control. Stagnation finds its roots in an exclusive desire for comfort. The zone in between is where the work of successful, sustainable change takes place. To the extent that we, as educators, adopt a collaborative ethic focused on teaching and learning, we develop our capacity to navigate between the Scylla and Charybdis of paralyzing fear and comfortable stagnation.

In addition, the power of beginning with questions as the way to engage educators and public alike in the work of meaningful school reform cannot be underestimated. They must be real questions, however, not the ones we think we already have answers to—which would make the collaboration inauthentic. And they must be appropriate questions. In his public Conversations, Bronson Alcott raised questions that only marginally advanced his students' academic learning while offending cultural norms.

Case Closed

Bronson Alcott was not shunned for *his views* on the divinity of Christ. Unitarian ministers and their precursors were doing that as far back as 1784. Rather, it was his exploration of those views as well as his views on other subjects either taboo in the New England culture of the times or not directly connected to schoolwork that raised public ire. Specifically, three transgressions repulsed the Boston intelligentsia and social elite: first, Alcott's exploration of sexual subjects with his pupils; second, the suspicion that he was abusing the classroom and his relationship with the pupils charged under him to proselytize his particular sectarian beliefs; and third, that he was stepping on the Unitarian clergy's theological turf—here was an amateur pretending to instruct in religious doctrine and proving to be such an embarrassment in the process. As he was an embarrassment for the liberal cause in Boston and fuel for their conservative critics, it became essential for the Unitarian clergy to distance themselves from Alcott.

In a broader context, what brought Alcott and his Temple School down might be summarized in Alcott's failure to anticipate the very foreseeable community fears that his controversial public statements would inspire. Had he not extended his Conversations to such taboo subjects as the divinity of Christ and human sexuality, and especially not published them in a book, his story might have turned out very differently. We might have found him advising Horace Mann on common school pedagogy in the 1840s during his tenure as commissioner of education instead of withdrawing both psychically and geographically first to Concord and then farther west to the little farming community of Harvard, where he isolated himself and his family at Fruitlands in 1842. Though there was less formal, centralized control in Boston in the 1830s than in other places or other times, there were still in place powerful community norms that Alcott brazenly violated. The clearest indication of this fact was that his allies—the Unitarian clergy—turned against him.

The precipitating force in Alcott's demise was community fear rooted in the biases of the day and Alcott's blithe violations of them. His public statements about Christ and human sexuality could easily have been avoided, and he would likely have continued on as a celebrated educator. His downfall is due principally to his failure to anticipate community concerns and his utter failure to value the success of his school enough to keep his mouth judiciously shut. Alcott's example reminds us all that fear is central to change, and that the ways in which we address, or fail to address, fear will powerfully influence outcomes.

The View from the Top

Framing the Issue

Many of us enjoy arranging things when we feel overwhelmed, such as desktops, files, or cupboards, because it helps restore a sense of order and control. It allows us to return to whatever situation was previously overwhelming us with renewed energy and interest. There is a related activity, which is not so helpful. It occurs when we confuse the real situation and the desktop. That is, we delude ourselves, when overwhelmed by an enormously complex task, into believing that it is appropriately resolved just because we have organized the desktop that covers it or the files that talk about it. This happens in education a lot. It occurs whenever any of us looks across the complex landscape of learning and concludes that if we can imagine a tidy system for managing it, then we will be well on our way to solving all related problems. The way in which we, as a nation, increasingly look at curriculum is unfortunately an example of this activity.

A good syllabus is a helpful thing for teacher and students alike. It clarifies goals, identifies key texts, provides a road map for the course, describes assignments and policies, and offers rubrics, all helpful things to know before the work begins. Like a building blueprint in the hands of a contractor or a trail guide in the hands of a hiker, it lets us know what our work is about and where we are supposed to end up. It allows us to proceed with sufficient confidence in the exploration of new terrain.

To be really useful, a syllabus should be designed to serve the learning of the student. This may appear to be an obvious truth, but it is lost in the contemporary policy world of curriculum development, where state frameworks, national council standards, and the implied curriculum of high- stakes tests have collided (perhaps colluded) to create a kind of metasyllabus for American K–12 education that is nothing short of disastrous. It is a system that mistakes the tidying impulse of files and desktops with the real work of engaging students in meaningful learning. With their enormous quantity of content and their lengthy lists of goals, these frameworks may look impressive to those at the top of the system and to the onlooking public, but in the classroom and the faculty planning room, where teachers strain to construct engaging lessons from too much material, they are a recipe for completely alienating a generation of young people from school. And they are, to a large extent, succeeding.

The origins of the nation's metasyllabus are complex, with roots in our nation's culture wars, other partisan/ideological debates, the increasing involvement of state and federal agencies in local K–12 curriculum and assessment, the highly politicized nature of curriculum creation, the so-called standards movement, and the ever-present fear factor so influential in American public education. (Fear finds current, potent expression in the widespread anxiety that China and India are getting ahead of the United States in engineering and technology.)

This chapter will not attempt to explain how the metasyllabus evolved; rather, what we will be discussing here is understanding a dynamic that works within and among the various forces identified above, as well as others. "The view from the top" is the tendency to impose plans that look great from above but that make little sense at ground level. Nowhere in education is this tendency more potently at work than in the areas of curriculum and assessment. As with the other cases spotlighted in the other chapters of this book, the case at the heart of this chapter features a school that has managed to break through the conspiracy against thoughtful schooling. In the case featured here, the Francis W. Parker Charter Essential School breaks through the conspirator that we call "the view from the top." From its inception, the Parker School has rejected solutions that are driven by adult needs for the appearance of order, control, and predictability and has, instead, been guided unswervingly by the learning needs of students. This is not to say that the school is chaotic! By no means. It is a safe and an orderly place, but it is a safety and an order that is defined by student learning. It may not be particularly quiet, but the noise is all about learning. The classrooms may not be the tidiest, but their apparent disarray is like the messiness of an artist's studio, where thoughtful and creative work is continually in progress. There are no lengthy lists of rules and consequences for misbehavior, but student and adult interactions are guided by an ethic of mutual respect and upheld by thoughtful interventions when that ethic is compromised.

The following section begins with a description of the Parker School's founding. This is followed by a slice-of-life narrative drawn from the school's early years. The narrative takes us on a tour of one curriculum cycle from planning to teaching to assessment, underscoring the continuous effort by the adults involved to shape their work to the needs of their students. The narrative is written from my perspective as a teacher in the school.

Case in Point

What if a small group of committed citizens was granted the opportunity to create its ideal school?[1] What if the state agreed to fund such an enterprise in exchange for a commitment that this school would be open to all children, regardless of race, household income, community of residence, or any other form of exclusion? What if, in this school, the minds and the aspirations of its students were taken very seriously, if each student was known well by at least one teacher, and if room was granted for students and teachers jointly to be led by their intellectual curiosity into a deeper understanding of the world and their relationship to it? What if . . . ?

The Francis W. Parker Charter Essential School was organized in response to the Massachusetts Education Reform Act of 1993, which called for the establishment of twenty-five "charter" schools, each fully public in both funding and access but each free to invent itself according to an idiosyncratic mission and design. The Parker School began with 120 students, ranging from age twelve to fourteen, drawn from thirty surrounding communities. Over the course of five years and a tiered- growth process, the school grew to enroll 350 students who matriculate through high school graduation.

All in a Name

The Francis W. Parker Charter Essential School is a particular school that has evolved in a particular place and time. It is unique, as all schools are, and yet the issues that define its work may be found in different form in almost any public secondary school in the nation. A look at the school's name reveals much about its particular identity.

"Parker"

To really understand the Parker School, we need to understand its philosophical roots. There has long been in American educational culture an impulse that spontaneously affirms the goodness and intelligence of children and values the child's natural curiosity by building its pedagogy around the child: lessons driven by student questions, and knowledge that is constructed from experimentation, inquiry, and dialogue. While this liberatory—or liberal—impulse has long been present in American educational culture, it has rarely—perhaps never—been the *dominant* impulse. It has played the underdog in a perpetual tug-of-war with a more powerful cultural conservatism, which sees human nature as essentially bad and knowledge as the acquisition of unwavering, universal truths. The kind of learning generated by this latter viewpoint seeks mainly to infuse the student with culturally accepted knowledge. Its methods are memorization, drill, and recitation.

The dominant impulse finds ready allies among our cultural conspirators. The manufacturing metaphor supports a mechanistic theory of knowledge in which facts and concepts are attached to minds. The fear factor is enlisted to keep the public simultaneously afraid that their way of life is at risk and that a tightly controlled educational system is their last best hope. The grand interlock of the industrial bureaucracy ensures that no innovation may gain an inroad to threaten the system. And the view from the top provides the psychological reassurance that all is well because all is neatly under control.

At different historical moments, the liberal impulse has surged and gained a solid foothold in the tug-of-war over influence in mainstream educational institutions and practice. Each time, however, it has ultimately been overwhelmed by the dominant cultural conservatism. One example of this liberal surging is the kindergarten movement inspired by Friedrich Froebel in Germany and popularized during the mid-1800s in the United States by Elizabeth Peabody (formerly Bronson Alcott's assistant at the Temple School) and others.[2] In the later 1800s, the torch was picked up by Francis Parker, whose work in the Quincy, Massachusetts, schools was profiled in chapter 2.[3] In the early 1900s, the work of the Progressive Education Association, inspired by John Dewey, and, in particular, its landmark Eight-Year Study (1933–1941), once again brought liberal ideals into the educational mainstream.[4] Since the 1980s, the work of the Coalition of Essential Schools, led by Theodore Sizer, has significantly altered practice in an ever-wider circle of schools across the nation and internationally as well.[5]

The Francis W. Parker Charter Essential School, in taking its name from Francis Parker, signals at once its connectedness to the pedagogy that Parker advocated and the liberal legacy that his name suggests. It also takes on the challenges inherent in a liberal educational stance taken in the midst of a conservative educational mainstream. This challenge provides a major theme in the curriculum discussion that follows.

"Charter"

Parker is a charter school, a peculiar species of public school spawned by state policy. In the 1990s, it was a species that found warm welcome in statehouse after statehouse and multiplied at lightning speed in urban, suburban, and rural communities.[6] Though its political enemies were numerous, its allies crossed political party lines and formed an effective ad-hoc coalition that generated ever-more charter schools in ever-more states.

Though policies establishing charter schools vary somewhat from state to state, the legislation that authorized the establishment of charter schools in Massachusetts, and with it the Parker School, is fairly typical of a strong charter school law. Under the Massachusetts Education Reform Act of 1993 and related regulations promulgated since, a group of individuals or an organization may submit a plan for a school to the state Department of Education. The plan must outline the school's mission, design, means by which the school will be held accountable for educational outcomes, facility plans, and so forth. The charter application is reviewed in a competitive process by the state Department of Education and is either authorized or rejected. The original Massachusetts legislation called for twenty-five charter schools, of which fourteen opened in September 1995. Parker is one of the original fourteen Massachusetts charter schools.

Massachusetts charter schools are public schools, supported by tax dollars, open to all students residing within the state, and accountable to such expectations as may be presumed of a public institution: church-state separation; nondiscrimination in matters of ethnicity, class, creed, disability, and sexual orientation; and tuition-free.

Once granted a charter, the school may solicit students and, once in operation, is reimbursed by the state for each student, an amount equal to the per pupil spending in the student's district of residence. For example, if Mary lives in school district A and her district spends $7,000 per student, then that is what the state reimburses the charter school for Mary's enrollment. At the same time, the school will receive $13,000 from the state for enrolling Eddie, who happens to live in school district B, which spends $13,000 per student. The school is subject to annual review by the state and must submit to a rigorous site inspection and five-year review in order to renew its charter, which expires every five years.

The justification for charter schools is manifold and will vary depending on the political/philosophical agenda of whichever advocate one may happen to question.[7] Several of the most often-stated justifications follow:

Parental choice: Charter schools grant families the power to exercise choice over the school their children attend. Such power, of considerable weight in and of itself, carries implications beyond the initial determination of which school is chosen. Having chosen once, parents may choose again. This is a fact that plays significantly into the planning of charter school operators, who know they must satisfy their clients or their clients will leave. Thus parental choice becomes both an end in itself and a means by which schools become authentically accountable to the families they serve.

Educational innovation: With each charter school enacting a unique design, the expression of an idiosyncratic mission, the whole field of charter schools becomes a great arena of diverse school innovations. Some ideas will flourish and catch on elsewhere, while others will prove unfruitful, the schools will close, and the children will move on.

Alternative education: For some, charter schools mean the opportunity to establish, within the public sector, schools of a known alternative nature: a Montessori school, perhaps, or a dropout prevention program based on principles of behavior modification.

Free markets: For some, charter schools represent the introduction of free-market principles into an arena characterized by entrenched bureaucracy and institutional stagnation. From this perspective, charter schools are seen as a catalyst that will electrify public education through competition for students and the revenue that each student represents.

Cost containment: Some see charter schools as a way of decentralizing and simplifying public education as a means of reducing public cost. Small schools that are organizationally flat, free of unions, and empowered to hire and fire staff will be more nimble and frugal with public monies.

The Parker School's early impetus sprang from local families who sought mainly an educational alternative for their children. The particular alternative they chose is signaled by the next word in the school's name.

"Essential"

The year 1984 marks the publication of a seminal work in the history of American education. *Horace's Compromise: The Dilemma of the American High School,* by Theodore R. Sizer, represented the findings of *A Study of Schools,* commissioned by the National Association of Secondary School Principals and the National Association of Independent Schools and led by Sizer. Horace, the fictional every-teacher of Sizer's book, lives a life of professional compromise indicative of the "genial mindlessness" of the American high school, portrayed through Horace's daily rounds of oversized classes and meaningless routine. A remedy is offered in the closing chapters, distilled into a compact list of five "imperatives," which, if thoughtfully enacted by communities, would, according to Sizer, catalyze a meaningful improvement of American secondary schools. The imperatives are:

1. Give room to teachers and students to work and learn in their own, appropriate ways.

2. Insist that students clearly exhibit mastery of their schoolwork.

3. Get the incentives right, for students and for teachers.

4. Focus the students' work on the use of their minds.

5. Keep the structure simple and thus flexible.[8]

Restless to proceed from writer's tablet to activist's stump, Sizer launched in 1984 the Coalition of Essential Schools from Brown University. Joined initially by a dozen schools and guided by a more fully articulated list of Common Principles, the Coalition of Essential Schools set sail. In the years since, it has grown into an international movement with over 1,000 member schools.[9]

In 1994, when the opportunity to establish charter schools in Massachusetts became a reality, several neighbors in the small town of Harvard, an hour's car ride northwest of Boston (and not affiliated with the university), considered taking on the challenge. Several of these neighbors were well acquainted with the Sizers, who owned a home in town. Thus it became clear early on that this would be a Coalition school. Indeed, Ted Sizer and his wife Nancy were recruited as trustees. As a brand-new school, Parker represented an opportunity to design, whole cloth, according to Coalition principles. There was no established school culture to challenge, and there were no long unquestioned practices to newly query, at least not in the most concrete sense of a school building where schooling was already under way. The Parker School would be a fresh start.

"School"

The most pervasive force in the day-to-day life of the school during its early years was the absence of history, that is, the overwhelming fact of the school's newness. There were no established policies, and there was no established culture, and yet, all of a sudden, there was a school filled with students and teachers, with a payroll and supplies, parents and athletic teams, classrooms and hallways, and toilets to be cleaned. The absence of history was at once a blessing and a burden. It promised a longed-for opportunity to start anew, to create something responsive directly to the needs of students, undistracted by preexisting contracts or entrenched practices. The viewpoint from which the school was created was not "from above." It was very much "on the ground."

Curriculum at Parker

We turn now to a narrative of the curriculum process at the Parker School taken from its early years. It is a process that deliberately rejects the tendency to impose plans that make sense from above and instead seeks to engage students directly, "at ground level." In what follows, we step right into the action, which takes place among students within the school's "Division 1," its youngest students, who are typically ages twelve to fourteen. They are at work with teachers in the school's interdisciplinary "arts and humanities" domain. The school is in its fourth year of existence. The narrative is told from a first-person perspective drawn from my own notes as a Parker School teacher at the time.

The Museum of World Cultures

The entire fall semester had been a massive drive toward a grand student exhibition: a museum of world cultures made up of approximately 150 individual exhibits, each one created by a Division 1 student and each one incorporating a semester's worth of learning. Each exhibit was assessed for artistic expression, research, and writing. As well, in the course of preparing for the exhibit, student work was assessed for reading, listening, and oral presentation.[10] To produce the exhibition, several curricular strands were woven together over a four-month period, from September to December. Students had learned about clay modeling, ancient hunter-gatherer cultures, early river valley civilizations, ancient Greek mythology, research skills, museum curatorship, and a single ancient or contemporary aboriginal culture of the student's choice, explored through a guided independent study. It was a lot, and viewed as a laundry list—"from the top"—it looked quite disparate, disconnected even. But, bound by the idea of the culminating exhibit, it cohered and made organic good sense at the ground level of student learning.

We introduced the museum idea to our students early in the year, explaining that most of what we were to do during the fall semester would be intended to prepare everyone to do a good job with their individual exhibits. This provided all with a concrete and meaningful purpose. This was the big pedagogical hook.

Our first step in September, on the way to our January exhibitions, was a look at hunter-gatherer cultures in an effort to understand basic societal needs in the context of the world's least complex societies. If basic human needs could be discerned, then surely these societies consisting of small, self-sufficient bands of forty to fifty people with few possessions and no permanent homes would draw them out in clear relief. The San people of the Kalahari Desert gave us our first glimpse of simple nomadism and challenged our collective sense as highly materialistic, mostly middle-class Americans of what one really needs to survive, indeed, what one needs to find fulfillment in one's daily living. We viewed selected portions of *The Gods Must Be Crazy* for its wry and provocative commentary on this very issue. We also reviewed literature on the recent discovery of the so-called Iceman, an almost perfectly preserved 5,000-year-old hiker who lost his way in the Italian Alps and remained frozen in a glacier until just a few unusually warm summers before when several skiers happened upon his partially exposed body. Complete with bow and quiver, thongs and jewelry, and a score of other personal effects, this late Paleolithic individual has provided a wealth of new data for paleoanthropologists. And our students thought the photos were "way cool."

To provide a theoretical framework for our studies, we drew on the ethnographic technique of dividing human culture into universal elements (family, governance, economics, education, etc.). A thoughtful listing of human needs that cross cultures allowed us to begin to compare hunter-gatherer societies with our own and ask why, if these early, simple societies were so successful, did they almost, without exception, evolve into agricultural communities and then urban societies with the discovery of agriculture? To assist us with this inquiry, we provided our students with a packet of short articles about key stages in the development of some of the major river valley civilizations of the Neolithic era: the Nile, the Tigris and Euphrates, the Indus, and the Yellow rivers. With title and other identifying details removed, students had to match each article to the correct civilization and then place the articles for each civilization in chronological order. "Where are the patterns?," we were asking, and, having solved the puzzles, what comparisons might one draw among the independent but highly parallel developments in all of the various regions? Why did all of these societies shift with apparent inevitability toward urban societies? Was it about satisfying basic human needs, or was there some kind of technological imperative that drove peoples everywhere toward infinitely greater complexity? Was it simply greed and the opportunity to gather and hold possessions that a settled way of life in permanent dwellings afforded? Was there a need that, despite appearances to the contrary, was left unmet by the uncomplicated ways of our Paleolithic ancestors?

These questions were the subject of regular discussion and became the basis of a major assessment that we designed for our students about a month into the semester. For this assessment, students had to pull together their experiences to date and tell the narrative of the Neolithic revolution in the form of a children's storybook. The book had to offer a theory for the adoption of agriculture, as well as illustrations. This work was assessed for writing and artistic expression.

At the same time we were exploring historical themes, we were also providing an introduction to clay sculpting. We had wanted to provide some sort of studio art experience, and, since clay was among the first materials manipulated for both practical and aesthetic ends, it seemed a logical choice. My teaching partner, Martha, who possessed experience as a potter, offered a master class to the Division 1 teaching team. The team consisted of six teachers, who worked in pairs, with each pair responsible for two groups of about twenty-five students each, making six classes total. From Martha, we learned basic terms such as wedging and throwing, basic properties of clay such as the fact that it shrinks by one-third as it dries, and, most importantly, we had a chance to work with clay ourselves. With Martha's tutelage, we then went forth and offered our initial clay workshops to our students. We coordinated our classes so the clay workshops all occurred on the same day, and Martha visited all of our classes to help guide the work. In a school that expects of its teachers a willingness to stretch beyond their areas of teaching comfort, it is also important that we support each other by sharing our individual areas of expertise. Martha not only provided us with a clay sculpting primer but also, with the aid of a slide presentation featuring upper Paleolithic art, she walked us through the crucial art history of the period we were studying. Students not only modeled with clay but also studied the caves at Lascaux, the Venus of Willendorf, and other early artistic works.

However, the clay workshops, or "clay days," as they became known by our students, were the big hit. We wanted our first session to be as original an encounter with clay as possible. We began with a visioning exercise that placed the class in a hunter-gatherer band 10,000 years ago. Imagine, we suggested, that you discover a new substance along the banks of the river one day as you are out for a walk. You tug a handful of the substance away from the ground and begin to explore its properties. At this point, we handed each student a wedge of clay and for one hour each student was to play with it as though it were the first time she or he had encountered it. The students' only responsibilities were to be sincere in their effort to maintain the pretense and then, at the end of the hour, to take twenty minutes to write an initial entry into what was to become a clay journal. The playful, and (moderately) purposeful chaos that ensued was a delight. In response to students' interest, we established a throwing wall, where all were free to hurl large or small pieces with as much force as they wished. We also designated a space on the floor for dropping. Some students with a more tactile sensibility squished it between their toes. Several tasted it (harmless). One attempted to extrude it through the gap in his front teeth. As the hour wore on, a strong gender pattern emerged. The boys were mostly hurling clay globs and crafting weapons, while the girls were shaping representational art and making pots. Shortly, we cleaned up, journaled for the promised twenty minutes, and then debriefed the experience, raising among several questions that of gender-based patterns. This led to a discussion of hunters and gatherers. Why do the roles fall sharply within gender lines? To what extent are behavioral patterns genetically influenced? To what extent are they culturally invented?

Several clay days were held during the fall semester. As students gained familiarity with the medium, we challenged them with increasingly focused tasks. Ultimately, they would be expected to create an original sculpture representing in some way the culture they would later choose to study. In the meantime, they regularly looked forward to the next clay day. "Are we having clay day today?" was the regular query at the beginning of class.

With a general background in early civilizations established by our river valley studies, we next wanted our students to carry out a more sustained inquiry into a single ancient culture to ready them for the independent study they would soon conduct. We chose Homeric and classical Greece, which would include a reading of the *Odyssey* and a focus on myth as a crucial mechanism for sense-making in human societies. Our month-long study was organized around a very activity-oriented reading of the *Odyssey*, supplemented with forays into Greek history and culture. The assignment that seemed to most capture everyone's imagination was the task of picking a favorite Greek myth or heroic tale and transforming it into a performance. For many students in their first year at Parker, the Greek myth performance was the first time they had been expected to perform solo before a live audience for an extended period.

Our *Odyssey* study coincided with a dramatic production staged at the Huntington Theater in Boston. Thus our daily rounds at Parker were punctuated by a day trip into the city for what turned out to be a minimalist interpretation of the great epic. The only props were long sticks, which the actors used variously as oars, swords, and architectural elements, and silk parachutes, which represented the boiling sea, fearful mountains, and narcotic dreamscapes. The play was particularly helpful in illustrating for our students, who were at that time readying their own myth performances, the power of imagination in conjuring up a scene with the fewest of props.

The various strands of our braided studies were coming together: historical knowledge, artistic skill with clay, performance experience. To take on the museum exhibition, two more strands needed to be added: museum curatorship and research. It so happened that the mother of one of our students was a museum curator. While her experience was mostly with natural history exhibits, she consented to present to each of our classes a workshop on the basics of exhibit design. And so she did, explaining how to integrate text, images, and objects into a presentation that would be both attractive and informative. Her presentation served also as a useful prep for the museum-based field trips on which we were about to embark.

We had considered during our summer planning the possibility of taking our students to several museums with the dual purpose of letting them experience some superbly designed exhibits and giving them the opportunity to "shop" for a culture they would make their own for the independent project. During the early part of the semester, we researched several possibilities and concluded that two trips were needed, one to New York, to the Metropolitan Museum of Art and American Museum of Natural History, and a second trip to Boston, to the Museum of Fine Arts and the Isabella Stewart Gardner Museum. Martha volunteered to make scouting trips to all of them and produced as a result a fine set of guides and activity sheets for each. Fortunately, we were able to assemble a sufficient number of parent chaperones to create small groups of six to seven students each. Our pattern in each of the museums was for each one of the seven or eight groups to begin in a different gallery and move at its own pace through a prescribed route. Keeping the groups small was crucial to avoid a cattle-herding mentality and to make the experience meaningful for each student. The groups' various tasks in each gallery—observing, sketching, answering questions—centered around exhibit strategies and culture shopping, with some attention paid as well to exhibitions that related to cultures they had studied.

The museum trips worked. Many students came away with an interest in a particular culture sparked by a particular exhibit. For others, the work we had done with the ancient river valley civilizations or with Greece came suddenly to life. For nearly everyone, of course, the bus ride was most memorable of all.

The final strand to be braided in was research, itself a bundle of sophisticated skills to be teased apart and carefully taught. Given our limited time and the fact that the curriculum under way was already ferociously complex, we needed to be strategic in our thinking about which aspect of research we would focus on.

The advent of the Internet has dramatically altered the way students approach research. The dogged pursuit of relevant articles through the *Reader's Guide to Periodical Literature* of a generation ago has been replaced with the much-improved but deceptively simple Internet search engine. A student whose worldly experiences have been confined mainly to school, the shopping mall, and the latest home computer game may not have the perspective needed to distinguish between a Web site posted by a junior high school student in Illinois and an article from a refereed journal authored by an eminent China scholar. Our first task, then, was to teach just that. Matt, a member of the Division 1 teaching team, located a number of Web sites about UFOs, ranging from popular conspiracy clubs, to a weirdo in the desert with a computer, to a university-based monitoring institute. Printouts from these various sites became the raw material for a series of lessons about Internet scholarship. During the course of the semester, our library began a subscription to a fee-based service providing access to proprietary materials, that is, a magazine index with both popular and scholarly entries, newspapers from around the world, and major encyclopedias, mostly available in full text online. Suddenly, our students' Internet universe, formerly limited to public domain documents, included legitimately published material. Another lesson was therefore designed around public and private domain issues.

Additional research lessons were offered in note-taking and documentation, both of which require reading. We discovered in the midst of our lessons that many of our students weren't reading very much. They seemed fascinated by the chase, that is, the Boolean puzzle that would lead them to the right sources—itself a worthy task—but having located what looked like relevant material, they would download reams of text and graphics, organize it neatly in folders, and *not* read it. This became apparent when we came to note-taking. Many students had no clue what they should note. We went back to basics and explained that since their research is guided by questions they have designed, the notes they take will be on information that is in some respect an answer to or further insight into one of their questions. The impulse among our students attempting to take notes for the first time would be to note the main ideas of an article. They had to be coached to acquire the habit of reading an article critically for the information they sought as opposed to the points the author wished to highlight. Often, the two might be quite different.

With research lessons, students began in earnest their independent research projects. As the reports began to get churned out, it seemed the semester's work started to come together. The papers were littered with references to cultural categories, exhibits from the Metropolitan Museum of Art, Mesopotamia, hunter-gatherer cultures, Greek myths, and so on. The final step was for each student to create a museum exhibit, drawing on his or her research and learning from the entire semester. Central to the exhibit would be the clay artifact. Our final "clay days" in early January were devoted to the design and sculpting of a piece that would in some way represent each student's chosen culture, either as a reproduction of an actual artifact or a symbolic representation of some aspect of the culture. Three days in January were set aside for the Division 1 museum, a span of time when the "downstairs vault" (one of our two large assembly rooms) as well as the three classrooms we regularly inhabit for our Division 1 classes would be filled with 150 student exhibits. As the exhibit days approached, excitement rose, and our usual sense of classroom order disintegrated. Student work was becoming highly individualistic, as each student attended to the idiosyncrasies of her or his own exhibit; there was no classwide lesson to be taught; all simply did what they had to do, which was different for each student. At the same time, our regular teaching space was no longer available; our classrooms were quickly being transformed into labrynths of student exhibits. We were, essentially, giving over control of our classes—rooms and all—to our students. It was a big leap of faith for us to let our often fidgety, sometimes rascally twelve- and thirteen-year-olds completely take over, and it was unnerving. But, by and large, they were purposeful in their work. They knew what they needed to do, and they knew that in a matter of days what they produced, individually and collectively, would be on display for anyone to see. Clearly some students made poor use of their time, for which appropriate interventions took place, but the vast majority were intently engaged.

For the museum to make sense to viewers, we had decided to designate each room as a region—the Americas, East Asia and Oceania, Africa, and so on. As the museum days drew close, we set hours both during and after school, including a final all-school session when advisories, composed of older students, visited the exhibit space. Division 1 students who were nearing their gateway (the final student exhibition for promotion to Division 2) were asked to sign up as a docent for one or more sessions.

Of course, while the museum exhibit was installed, we still had to conduct our classes, a physical impossibility given that our classroom space was in use. It was partly in response to this fact but also as part of our deliberate planning that we decided our students should use this time to learn from each other. We therefore developed museum guides, much as we had for our New York and Boston trips, and then we sent students out in small groups to visit and study their classmates' exhibits. What patterns did they see within and across regions?

In addition to the academic learning that took place during the museum days, our students clearly took great pride in their accomplishment. It was an impressive display for both its enormous size and minute detail, as many visitors remarked. Perhaps the greatest moment occurred on the final day, when all of the older advisories were instructed to attend the exhibit. Each of the

Division 1 students stood by his or her work ready to explain, as the great and powerful Division 2 and Division 3 students browsed, paused to study, and asked questions, and, with laudable frequency, offered complimentary remarks. The viewing session was followed by a discussion consisting of paired advisories, one older, one younger, organized around the school's essential question for the year: Where are the patterns? As it turned out, the discussion was as much about the essential question as it was about older students admiring out loud the quality of work they saw in their younger peers' exhibits.

Larger Lessons

Viewed from above, this curricular unit does not make sense. Written up as a unit outline, it would appear scattered and incoherent. Observed in action by an uninformed visitor, the classroom would appear chaotic and the students unruly. And, as preparation for a standardized test, it would be grossly ill-fitting. Viewed at ground level, from the vantage point of student learning, student engagement, and teacher practice, it *does* makes sense. The learning goals are clear, and the performance standards are explicit in schoolwide documents and assignment-specific rubrics. Student activities flow logically and build on one another. Instructional practice is continually adapted as plans devised in advance meet up with students in the act of learning. Though far from perfect, it stands as an example of what can happen when plans and designs are driven by the goal of student engagement as opposed to the planners' psychological needs for order, control, and predictability.

Realistically, however, if you work in a mainstream public school, the preceding narrative may feel distantly outside of the realm of possibility. Our freedom to invent curriculum at the Parker School was enabled by a newly hired staff eager for adventure, an administrative team equally disposed to experimentation, a parent community assembled around a school of choice, and an explicitly progressive school mission. You may not enjoy such advantages in your setting. Were this chapter's "Case in Point" offered as *the* exemplar for all schools to follow, this narrative would be headed in a very unrealistic direction. But it is not offered as "the" exemplar. It stands instead as the expression of one public school's efforts in a very specific context involving a particular set of policies and a particular community of educators, parents, and students. It offers just one instance of a school defying the cultural norm of plans and designs driven by the designer's need for order and control and replacing it with a focus on student engagement. What you accomplish will look different based on your context, your approach, and your goals. Each school situation involves both impediments that keep you from doing what you want to do and opportunities that grant you the space to achieve your goals. You can quickly become depressed if you dwell on the impediments. In your zone of influence, do what you can in the space you have. At the edges of your zone of influence, push against the impediments that are set before you. As a citizen, advocate for radical, systemic change.

In the next three sections of this chapter, we examine three scenarios focusing on classroom practice, adult collaboration, and public engagement. Each one contrasts the strong cultural inclination to plan on the basis of adult needs with the possibility of shifting to a planning habit driven instead by student engagement and student learning.

Classroom Encounters

"Okay, everybody, please open your textbook to page 497. Today we're going to cover the Vietnam War. This came after the Korean War and was part of the Cold War. Key terms are on the board."

This opening to a high school social studies class will sound familiar to anyone who has taught high school or visited high school classrooms. The forty-five minutes of instruction are framed by what topic needs to be "covered" and related "key terms." The lesson for the day derives from the unit of study filling probably several weeks and "covering" a certain broader topic and wider expanse of time. This lesson may be embedded, for example, in a unit of study called "The Cold War," spanning 1947 to 1989. The unit of study in turn represents a portion of the yearlong plan, which is likewise defined topically ("America since the Civil War"). The mind-set that stands behind this approach to curriculum is driven by epistemological assumptions that run contrary to pretty much everything we know about the way people learn, from John Locke in the 1600s to Lev Vygotsky in the twentieth century. Here it is: facts and concepts can be dumped into minds.

Only they can't; our minds are simply too smart. Our minds interact with their environments through sensory/emotional experience and construct their own understandings about the world. Believing that we can dump information into young minds doesn't make it so. Unfortunately, many of us, despite common sense, despite our own experience of the world and despite everything that psychology tells us, persist in teaching methods based on the epistemology of dumping. When the teacher's erroneous belief in the epistemology of dumping meets up with the reality of a child's creative mind, what happens is often a nasty collision. While the teacher may believe the facts are pouring into the empty vessel in an orderly fashion, what is actually occurring is quite different. Even if certain surface narratives are being scripted in the student's head, the child is constructing her or his own deeper and more lasting narrative to surround it. The deeper narrative may be, for example, "These words are meaningless. I will memorize them like lines in a play in order to perform them." Or, "This activity is not only boring, it is insulting. I refuse to play along." Or, at the end of the day, "History is such a boring subject; it's all about memorizing worthless facts." Meanwhile, the teacher observes student apathy, docile compliance, or active rebellion and thinks, "What is wrong with these kids! In my day . . ." Meanwhile, students are mediating the experience, each one in her or his own way. Jamal in the front row: Okay, this information is meaningless, but I care about succeeding and grades are the path to success, so I will commit these meaningless facts to memory, recite them on the test, and then forget them. Jennifer in the back of the room: This work is utterly without meaning. I rebel quietly against the meaninglessness of it and put my head down. Henry near the bank of windows at the side of the room: I am so frustrated by the stupidity of this work that I have to do something else—anything else—to engage my mind, so I will talk with the person next to me about last night's game, and I will poke at the student in front of me with my pencil point and create a small drama. Tina, front and center: "So this is history. I like memorizing things, and I'm good at it. If I memorize lots of this and can put it on a time line, maybe I could be a historian." In any of these cases, the metalearning of the student is an unfortunate and a very logical conclusion based on his or her classroom experience.

But you are decidedly *not* like the teacher described above. You understand how children learn, you value the structure of your discipline, be it history or mathematics or something else. And yet you are constrained, like the teacher above, by curriculum mandates created by others who just don't get it! What do you do? The answer, as with so much in combating the cultural conspirators against thoughtful schooling, is deceptively simple: you do what you can.

Suggestions:

1. Although the curriculum you have been handed may be driven by the impulse to cover content, you can introduce elements into your lesson that are driven by a desire to engage students. Even if the curriculum is jam-packed, there are small ways that you can shift the dynamic away from coverage and constructively toward student engagement. Are you teaching about the Vietnam War? Begin by asking students: Does a war protestor provide aid and comfort to the enemy or serve as a nation's conscience? Taking just three minutes to discuss that question with students, then linking it to the American experience of the Vietnam War, will provide something of a mental frame for students, around which they can assemble the information into their own intellectual construct—even if the balance of the class is the driest recital of information imaginable.

2. Shift the class away from teacher talk. If we learn best what we say and do ourselves, then construct your lessons in such a way that the students who are talking have appropriate opportunities to move about. Small groups designed around the host of cooperative learning techniques that have been developed over the last twenty years accomplish this shift ably.[11]

3. Build on your own positive experiences. Ask yourself: When were my students most engaged this year? What was going on in class? How can I build on those experiences? When did my students produce their best work—in terms of quality learning? When and how did I make adjustments that responded to student needs and student learning? Make a mental note of your answers to these questions and replicate the experiences in future lessons.

4. Don't be a slave to the textbook. Even if you have no control over the textbook choice, you likely have some control over how the textbook is used from day to day. You don't need to be a slave to the narrative or the chapter questions. Determine your goals and your approach to each lesson, and then draw on the elements of the text that best serve those needs. Have students read sections in the order that makes sense for your approach. Design your own reading questions. Use photos and graphics to serve your own ends. Supplement the text with short readings that illuminate an important point or that call a statement in the textbook into question or that approach a concept in the textbook from a different angle. Doing so will appropriately shift the role of the textbook from unquestionable gospel to helpful and incomplete resource.

Teacher Talk

"What we need here are some clear and unambiguous rules so everybody knows where we stand. These kids may be the product of permissive parents, but when they're here at school, they're ours, and we have rules, damn it! It's what kids want and need. Structure. Order. They're crying out for it. Woodlawn Middle School has a simple code of conduct that lists all possible offenses, and, for each one, it lists the penalty for the first offense, the second offense, the third offense, and so on. Everybody's clear, and the school is orderly!"

Earth science teacher Wayne Gallagher is emphatic. Behind his words stand thirty-seven years of school experience. His perspective is very understandable. He has 130-plus students to manage in five classes a day. He gets three minutes between classes to go to the bathroom or get ready for his next class. He corrects papers endlessly. He needs to cover content and keep his classes moving at a brisk clip through the curriculum. Wayne's workload requires careful and expert management, which he has mastered over his many years in the classroom. Dealing with student misbehavior on top of everything else is something he does not need. What he does need, to maintain his sanity, is well-regulated systems both in his classroom and in the school generally. A schoolwide code of conduct would help. This is what Wayne needs, and he has designed systems for his work and advocates systems for the management of the school that place a high priority on predictability, order, and control.

Wayne is not very different from any of us, except maybe in his degree of vehemence. We all feel empathy for his perspective, and yet Wayne's position feels harsh. Though admirable in some ways, it is not the kind of environment in which we would want our own child, especially if our own child is not a perfectly mature and well-behaved student. Consider the word "conduct" in code of conduct. Conduct speaks to observable behavior. As such, it frames the way we think about students for whom such a code would be devised. It suggests that our work with students in schools is about observable behavior: achieving the behaviors we want and extinguishing the behaviors we don't want. It defines our problems and our solutions strictly in terms of rules, rewards, and punishments and stimulus and response. The goal is a "behavior." The method is a "reward" or "consequence." Presumably, the successful graduate of such a school would "behave" and respond predictably to the offer of rewards and the threat of punishments and would function best when there are clear rules.

But what happens when this graduate steps out of the protective universe of his or her school and enters a world in which there is no single expectation of "behavior," where good behavior in one context is bad behavior in another; where good deeds often go unrewarded; where cheating and lying often go unpunished; where right conduct and right behavior are not nesessarily clear and unambiguous and must be carefully reasoned; where the list of rules differs from place to place; where some places have no rules; where the appearance of good conduct may be a masquerade for cruel intent? To the extent that we focus exclusively on conduct and behavior in schools, our graduates will be ill prepared for such a world.

So what, then, *do* we focus on while simultaneously ensuring that schools are safe and orderly places? We are moral beings. We judge and evaluate. We ponder what is good and true and beautiful. We possess the capacity for both compassion and cruelty. Our schools inevitably provide a moral education. We may deny it, but it is not possible to avoid it. The issue is whether the moral education we provide is appropriate to who we are and how we think and feel as a species, or not. Our schools can engage, exercise, and enhance the capacity of our students to judge and to reason, or they can cultivate cynicism while allowing their moral muscles to atrophy. A code of conduct that focuses strictly on behavior, rules, rewards, and punishments is inappropriate, because it neither engages nor exercises nor enhances our students' capacity to judge and to reason. It provides a mis-education. A moral education that is appropriate to the way people think and feel and act must teach us to judge and evaluate well, to ponder thoughtfully on the good, the right, and the beautiful, to exercise our capacity for compassion, and to understand very well our potential for cruelty. As with so much else in schools, a code of conduct looks good from above; it satisfies the adults' psychological need for order, control, and predictability, but at the ground level of student learning, it is dangerously misaligned with the way we think and act as a species.

Let's return to Wayne, whose situation is not unlike our own and whose frustrations we understand. Must we now add "moral education" to the list of required courses? Is this yet another requirement on top of all the other requirements? No it is not. It is something at once simpler and harder to achieve. It is not a new program but a fundamental shift in our thinking that permeates all aspects of our work with children and youth. Instead of making plans and designs driven by our psychological needs as adults for order, control, and predictability, we must make plans and designs driven by the goal of student learning, learning that includes a recognition that, whether we want to or not, we do provide a moral education in schools. It can be a good one or a bad one. It's up to us. Here are some suggestions for what you can do as a faculty.

1. When discussing the school's legitimate needs for order and safety, ask: How can the systems we design introduce our students, in an age-appropriate way, to judging what is right and why? How can the school's need for order and safety align with the school's central mission to engage students in meaningful learning?

2. When discussing the school's overall climate, avoid the narrow and superficial focus on "student behavior" and frame the conversation in terms of relationships: student to student, student to adult, adult to adult. How would you characterize these relationships? Where and when, in your school, are they caring and respectful? What are the settings in which that happens? What are the attitudes of the persons in those settings? How can those circumstances be cultivated elsewhere in the school?

3. Problematize the notion of student behavior. Identify a scenario in which an intervention by an adult is called for, and discuss what course of action by an adult in that situation would find the greatest balance between teaching and maintaining safety, between the press of multiple demands that every adult in school feels and the responsibility of an adult to pay attention to a small crisis. Quite likely, different adults in the group will offer different approaches, and the variations will offer an opportunity to crack open the simple shell of "discipline" and reveal its complex interior. As a faculty, ask: Do the existing practices in the school support the right balance? What would it take to achieve the right balance? What can be done within the system as it currently stands?

4. Engage students in the work of cultivating an orderly and a safe school environment. Most schools have a student government already in place. Most schools have homerooms, which are existing venues for jointly engaging students and adults in conversation regarding vital questions that center on the culture of the school that all of you share. With some careful planning and sensitivity to the dynamics of such conversations, the culture of a school can begin to move toward an appropriate moral education of its youth and a safe and an orderly environment.

Public Engagement

"One of the advantages of regionalization is that our high school will be able to offer a much broader range of courses." Paul Gallagher, school board member of the district in which you work, is making a point. As the assistant superintendent for curriculum and instruction, you find yourself mostly listening to Paul and the others at a committee meeting of the newly established Joint Committee for Regionalization. Your district and a neighboring district are considering merging. Both districts are small and struggling with increased special education costs, climbing facilities costs for the maintenance of aging buildings, and declining voter appetite for school spending increases. Several school board members from each town recently introduced the idea of regionalization as a way to achieve greater efficiency through economy of scale. There appears to be a groundswell of support for the idea across both communities. To the fiscal advantages, board members are now adding the image of curricular benefits. Board member Paul continues: "Currently the high school is unable to offer the full range of AP courses, art classes, science electives, and other programs. We're just too small. Regionalization would address that."

Diane Robbins, fellow board member and regionalization proponent, speaks next: "I have here copies of the high school course catalogue for Middle Valley Regional High School." Diane passes the glossy, substantial- looking booklets around the table of board members and central office staff from both schools. "If you flip through it, I think you will be impressed with the range of courses offered in many different subjects." The table falls quiet for a moment as committee members scan the catalogue. Heads begin to nod in approval as members scan the impressive array of course descriptions.

While you don't say much at the meeting, it leaves you with a vague feeling of discomfort. There's nothing wrong with greater efficiency, and the course book for Middle Valley is truly impressive looking. And yet Middle Valley has some problems. The high school has gone through three principals in the last six years. Last June, a drunken brawl broke out on the dance floor of the senior prom. A good friend who works as a guidance counselor at Middle Valley has complained for years that kids get lost there. And the local newspaper has been awash lately with angry letters to the editor about a "No hats" policy recently instituted at Middle Valley. The course catalogue looks good to board members sitting around a conference table. And it no doubt looks good to parents and incoming freshmen when it arrives in the mail in August. But the features that look so good from a distance have a different feel at the ground level of the individual student experience.

Students in large schools often feel emotionally disconnected from their educational experience. The monumental "Study of High Schools," which spawned Theodore Sizer's seminal work, *Horace's Compromise,* in 1984, clearly identified the anonymity of students in large, warehouse-like schools as the destructive norm in American secondary education.[12] These were schools with impressive course catalogues. Arthur Powell's *Shopping Mall High School*, published several years later, created the apt metaphor that stuck.[13] Big high schools with impressive elective programs are like shopping malls with lots of stores. You may amble genially among the aisles, even while you remain anonymous and emotionally disconnected. Sizer and Powell reminded us of the special importance of connectedness in schools, not just because it is nice, but because it is essential to learning. Connectedness in schools calls to mind the ecological metaphor for learning. Interdependence is at the center of an ecological worldview. No organism stands alone but depends on and is depended upon by other organisms. In isolation, we die. Denise Pope, an educator based in California, spent several months tagging along with five teenagers as they attended school and went about their lives. Her terrifyingly sad portraits rendered in the book *Doing School* remind us that two decades after *Horace's Compromise*, American students across all demographics remain disconnected from the large high school experience, which continues to be the American norm.[14]

But there is hope. The small school movement spawned by the pioneering work of Sizer's Coalition of Essential Schools during the 1980s and 1990s has been a promising response to the call for connectedness. While small schools have been advocated unrealistically in some quarters as the magic remedy for public education's multiple ills, more thoughtful practitioners have embraced the notion of small scale as the chief means of achieving the goal of stronger connections among teachers, students, and families. Experiments by school leaders committed to the importance of student connectedness have made stunning progress in student achievement gains. The Boston Pilot Schools effort launched in the early 1990s has shown dramatic educational gains, particularly among urban students who have struggled against long odds.[15] Three small high schools in New York City, featured in Jacqueline Ancess's *Beating The Odds*, demonstrate similarly how schools get it right when the quality of the individual student's experience becomes the basis of school design, curriculum development, and daily instruction.[16] My profiles of the Parker School (*Upstart Startup*) and the Bethlehem Lab School (*The School Inside Us*) speak as well to the efficacy of teachers who work in more intimate school settings that choose to focus on relationships and rigor.[17]

But back to you and the regionalization meeting. How do you respond to the twin attractions of economy of scale and course selection? More generally, how do you respond to the public when its impulse for school decisions is distracted by the proverbial view from the top without consideration of the impact at the ground level of the individual student's experience? Here are two simple suggestions.

1. Ask: How do we ensure that in this bigger school with more course options, kids don't feel lost? Ask: What do we know about the quality of learning in some of the large high schools with which we are familiar?

2. Point out that giving students opportunities to explore their interests can also be achieved in small schools with independent projects, senior capstone experiences, and flexible schedules that allow for cross-enrollment with nearby colleges. Indeed, small schools may be able to provide even greater opportunities for students to pursue their individual interests than the elective courses of a comprehensive high school.

Countering the Culture

The dominant culture of curriculum creation says more, more, more. More content, more facts, more concepts, more terms, more topics, more units of study, more courses. Such is the impulse from the view from the top, but at the ground level of student learning, more means less. It's even truer in today's world of weighty curriculum frameworks than it was in 1984, when Ted Sizer first reminded us that "less is more."

So how do we counter the culture of more? How do we identify what the curriculum ought to be about if it is not about the politicized phenomenon of curriculum creation that takes place in the Department of Education Committee Rooms?

It is difficult to tease apart the complementary notions of "skill" and "content." It is absurd to imagine learning any skill associated with, say, research that would not necessarily acquaint the learner with some body of knowledge. It is equally absurd to imagine learning how to read without *reading something*. It is possible, however, to imagine memorizing the dates of the Civil War without learning any meaningful skills connected with research or reading. These simple truths seem to be at the heart of contrasting approaches to curriculum development. Curricula focusing on "content" (the kinds of detailed state mandates that increasingly dominate the educational landscape) crowd out the meaningful learning of skills. In contrast, curricula that primarily assess skill development *will necessarily include* content, as the world cultures project described earlier illustrates. The "content camp" (it is unfortunately apt to express the issue in polarized terms) is frustrated by this approach, however, because a skills-based curriculum inevitably "covers" less content and denies the central authority power in preselecting the content to be studied and robs it of the opportunity to craft simple, standardizable tests. The problem to centralizers, then is not that a skills approach excludes content. Rather, the problem is that a skills approach frustrates the politically easy but educationally unsound inclination to include more content than could ever be meaningfully considered, and to dictate to communities what that content will be.

What content should we include? Two problems immediately arise. A roomful of reasonable people will quickly generate a list that exceeds the capacity of a school to teach or students to learn—really learn—unless the goal is mere acquaintance with content, memorization of factoids as opposed to deep understanding. The second problem is that a roomful of people representing the ethnically, economically, religiously, and philosophically diverse mosaic that our nation consists of will likely not agree on a reasonable list. Why, the daughter of Cambodian refugees will argue, should the Holocaust get more attention than Pol Pot's Killing Fields? Why, voices for gender equity will argue, should the literary canon include only the usual male names? Thoughtful scholarship is increasingly bringing to our attention women authors previously overlooked by a male-controlled literary establishment. But why, other reasonable voices will argue, should Shakespeare be pushed aside simply to make room for previously disregarded authors?

The reasonable conversation quickly degenerates into bickering and intellectual turf protecting. The path of least resistance is simply to include it all—a solution that ends the bickering among the adults but leaves the students and their teacher with an impossible task!

What, then, is essential? If there are skills, then there must also be content, the reasoning goes. If we write, then we write *about* something. If we listen, then we listen *to* something. And so on. The question is, does it matter what the content is? Mick Jagger or Mozart? Shakespeare or a clever Budweiser ad?

To press this question, we might take some generally undisputed entry to the content "canon" and ask whether it truly is essential and why. How about Shakespeare? Why should we read (or view or act) Shakespeare? The answer might include the following: Reading Shakespeare teaches us a good deal about the structure and history of the English language. Reading Shakespeare confronts us compellingly with certain themes universal to human experience (conflict, power, love). Reading Shakespeare teaches us a good deal about rhetoric, style, and literary conventions. Reading Shakespeare is a joy, a rewarding aesthetic experience in and of itself. Reading (or, better, acting) Shakespeare teaches us about movement and oral expression. Reading Shakespeare acquaints us with the origin of certain common phrases ("A rose by any other name . . .") and common allusions (Romeo and Juliet) that grant us access to the cultural-linguistic mainstream.

All of these answers suggest that the end is not Shakespeare's texts themselves but some more abstract ends that Shakespeare's plays and sonnets happen to serve: the history and structure of the English language, aesthetics, universal human themes, cultural literacy, and so on. That we choose Shakespeare as the means to these ends is not automatic but rather an acknowledgment of Shakespeare's genius, that is, his work gives us entree to so much that we care about. This same logic could be extended to anything else in the arts and humanities that one might place on a list of "essential content," for example, Mozart or Michelangelo or Huck Finn or E. D. Hirsch's infamous "vestal virgins." They are on the list not for their own sake but because their presence there serves a more abstract end.

All of this seems to suggest that if we really want to identify what is essential about essential content, it will not be long lists of famous books and famous dead people, the choice of which we bicker endlessly about. Rather, what is essential are those further ends that our lists serve.

What are the further ends? Here, very tentatively suggested, is a schema based on the "further ends." It divides essential content into two broad categories: "ways of knowing" and "universal themes of human experience." The so-called ways of knowing tend to constitute the basic tools/language/elements of the academic disciplines. They represent the manifold ways that we take in the world, the means by which we process experience. The second category, universal themes of human experience, is just that—big, recurring ideas that cross regions and epochs. Here's what a partial attempt at the list might look like:

Essential Arts and Humanities Content:

1. Ways of knowing (the means by which we take in the world): principles of design (visual art); causality, chronology, periodicity (history); grammar and rhetoric (language); literary genres (literature); culture (anthropology); tonality, harmony, melody (music); production and distribution of resources (economics); and so on.

2. Themes of human experience (big, recurring ideas that cross regions and epochs): change, community, beauty, truth, conflict, love, and so on.

Does all of this mean we don't teach Shakespeare or Mozart (or Mick Jagger or Budweiser ads)? On the contrary, there will be plenty of "stuff" that we teach, including probably many of the usual things (Shakespeare, the Revolutionary War, slavery, Michelangelo), as well as many less usual things (the U'Wa, Star Power, Zlata Filipovic). We are not bound, however, by anyone's (not even our own) list of such things. Instead, we are bound by a list of the ends to which we might teach Zlata or William Shakespeare. That is, we do not warrant that our graduates will know authors X, Y, and Z together with wars A, B, and C. Rather, we warrant that our graduates will be able to explain principles of design, apply their knowledge of the production and distribution of resources, and discourse on the nature of conflict in the human experience. It is up to us, the teachers, in consultation with our own community, to wisely choose the topics or foci of our students' work to ensure experiences rich enough to truly exercise their capacities in these areas. A great playwright like Shakespeare might tend to get chosen because his work provides ample material across so many categories. But the Budweiser ad could conceivably get some airtime too, depending on our purposes. The choices remain fluid, but their selection is not arbitrary; it is guided by an ambitious list of capacities that we seek to cultivate in our students. If we expect our students to become proficient with those capacities on our list in the few short years that they are with us, then we must choose our studies wisely.

Is Shakespeare essential? The answer is no. What, then, *is* essential? The answer is aesthetics and design, causality and harmony, the good, the true, and the beautiful.

Case Closed

There has been pressure over the years for the Parker School to add more "content" to its skill-oriented learning standards. But to identify even one person or document or event as crucial (excepting perhaps the U.S. Constitution) is to begin a wearisome and an ultimately futile process. If a student were to graduate from the Parker School lacking familiarity with a particular author, then it would be because for six years a dozen reasonably capable scholars working responsively with the school community felt it was not the most important thing for her to learn. Better to rely on the dynamic judgment of scholars in action than some calcified canon (defined at a particular moment by a particular group of people for all time) with which we may not tamper because of the self-serving sacredness of the list. Better to create and assess the value of curriculum by its ability to meaningfully engage students than by adult needs for order and control.

The Grand Interlock

Framing the Issue

The school-within-a-school is a well-known kind of innovation. Carving a smaller learning community out of a larger, existing school has been a favored approach for a variety of purposes: alternative programs for students at risk of failure, elite programs for "gifted" students, progressive options for families restless with convention, and laboratories for experimental treatments.

The school-within-a-school also has a reputation for trouble. More than other school reform options, it places the reform in close and often abrading proximity to whatever is not being reformed. The innovation doesn't mesh with the gears of the surrounding system. It shouldn't, after all, because it is intended to run according to a different design. But because it is nested within the larger system, a workable interface must be crafted, or something will be sure to break down. Framed in a different metaphor, one might think of the school-within-a-school as a transplanted organ for which the possibility of tissue rejection is high. Careful, vigilant attention and a regimen of antirejection drugs are needed!

The trouble that a school-within-a-school generates makes it a perfect subject for our exploration of the Grand Interlock—the tendency of the system to crush promising innovation. The Bethlehem Lab School, with which I was associated as founder and then director, is a school-within-a-school. Its genesis was the restlessness of a circle of colleagues with the conventional school practice that surrounded us. Its gestation and rocky infancy offer insight into the challenges that innovation faces from all directions by the larger system. Its development suggests, also, the means by which a functional interface may be crafted to protect work that challenges the status quo.

Case in Point

Good ideas for school reform are easy to come by.[1] The greater challenge lies in translating good ideas into practice and getting them to stick. In the summer of

1988, a group of teachers in the Bethlehem Central School District in upstate New York met to deliberate on a body of then-current school reform literature to see how it might relate to our students. We developed plenty of good ideas and dreamed wistfully of transforming our schools. That was the easy part. Over a period of several years, a number of us attempted to implement just a few of those ideas and found that, while we experienced some success, the institutional barriers to change were enormous. Nonetheless, through a combination of luck, well-placed allies, and inventive thinking, we were able to find a space among the larger gears of the system in which the smaller gears of our program could turn in ways that served students well.

In the spring of 1988, a group of teachers requested that the district fund a summer committee to review literature on school reform and to develop a kind of think tank report to the faculty and staff. The district funded our request, and we met for a week that summer to review the recent work of John Goodlad, Theodore Sizer, Ernest Boyer, Mortimer Adler, and others. We produced a report that was distributed to all district staff members. The week of discussion and the development of the report were stimulating exercises, but they did not directly result in any changes in school practice.

The following spring, a number of us decided to act, in a small way, to begin to change our practice. We developed a team teaching pilot project that was to pair two English classes with two social studies classes in two consecutive periods. One English class and one social studies class would be held with separate teachers during the first of the two periods. For the second period, the students in the English class would go to the social studies teacher and the students in the social studies class would go to the English teacher. In this way, two teachers and two classes of students would have a dedicated double period that they could reconfigure at will. We designed an interdisciplinary course that was made possible by the new flexibility of the scheduling innovation. When the program was formally announced in June, some members of the faculty expressed resentment that they were being presented with a fait accompli. Why hadn't they been asked for their ideas? How would this affect class size for teachers not involved in the project? Wisely or unwisely, we forged ahead through the thick underbrush of faculty questions and uncertainties. To our dismay, when we returned in September to begin the project and were given our class lists, we found that the paired classes were not perfectly paired. Some students were in one class but not the other. Attempts to remedy this inconsistency during the first two weeks of the school year caused only more irritation among the faculty, and we feared it might adversely affect the students. We scuttled the project. We had failed to anticipate and address the ways in which the innovation would grind against the gears of the larger system, and we had failed to anticipate and address a host of fears among our colleagues that the spectre of this innovation raised.

The next move was both naïve and illogical. I had concluded that the team teaching innovation flopped because it necessarily interfered with other programs. Lock fifty students into two periods of the day and you send a ripple effect throughout the master schedule. Some classes grow too big, while others shrink. Students get locked out of their favorite elective: chorus, band, technology. I began to imagine that the only sort of innovation that could succeed would be one that operated wholly apart from the existing master schedule. What if we were to create an entire school programmatically apart from but physically situated within the existing high school? It would be a school with its own students, its own teachers, and its own space carved from the larger high school space. To imagine that such a program would *not* grind against the gears of the larger system was indeed naïve, and to suggest that we overcome the failure of a small innovation by instituting a larger innovation was utterly illogical. Nonetheless, we moved ahead, because against the illogic of logistics stood the logic of desire and discontent. There were enough teachers, school administrators, and community members hungry for change. Where there was a will, we might also find a way.

What follows is a narrative of the birthing of the Bethlehem Lab School, an innovation that survived its infancy despite some naive assumptions because of a willingness to move more slowly and inclusively and a number of appropriate strategic moves that helped craft a workable interface between the lab school and the larger system.

In the fall of 1989, I approached the district duperintendent with a proposal to look into the development of a laboratory high school—a kind of alternative school with an experimental/progressive focus open to all students. He expressed interest in the idea but suggested that evidence of support would be crucial before the district could explore it. I decided then that I would approach the teachers' union with the idea. Union support and faculty support were crucial, as I had learned from the failed team teaching project.

I began to promote the idea at union meetings, conducted an informal interest survey among the high school faculty, and brought the results, which were favorable, back to the superintendent. Budding faculty support came with an important caveat: the faculty insisted on a vote prior to implementation. I sensed hesitancy to the idea of a faculty vote from the administrative team, but they nonetheless gave the green light to formal exploration of a laboratory high school. It was now October 1990.

We organized a design team of interested teachers and administrators. The team's immediate goal was to develop a grant proposal to fund the design work. This turned out to be an important exercise not only for raising needed money but also for clarifying our concept of the emerging lab school. We needed clear and simple design principles that we could use to describe the project to potential funders. Our deliberations yielded the following conceptual framework for the school: (1) an interdisciplinary focus to foster coherence for student learning; (2) an emphasis on fewer subjects studied in greater depth in order to build deeper understanding; (3) a project orientation to promote student initiative and personal relevance; (4) a focus on community building, with elements of democratic governance to build interpersonal skills and civic-mindedness; and (5) a commitment to operate the school within existing per pupil costs.

Our grant proposal was ready in April 1991, and we began circulating it immediately to a limited number of foundations where we had some sort of entrée. In June, the Klingenstein Fund in New York offered a generous matching grant. On the strength of that, the district superintendent and I took the grant proposal door to door among several corporate facilities located in our town. Owens-Corning, Roure Corporation, and General Electric provided generous donations, and, with the Klingenstein grant, we now had the funding we needed to move into the design phase. Also, with the funding support from outside parties, we gained a measure of credibility among colleagues and townspeople.

We reassembled the design team and enlarged it to include teachers from academic departments that were previously not represented. We were eighteen in all, and we faced the daunting task of designing, within a year's time, a lab school that would simultaneously honor the design principles and address the many swirling practical concerns regarding fitting into our existing programs. Initially uncertain about how to organize ourselves, a plan emerged from our discussion. We decided to divide the team into three small groups. Each group would serve as an independent design team. Each team was given the assignment of designing a lab school by March of the following year. Several small groups working independently, we reasoned, would be more functional and would yield a variety of ideas from which we could choose the best. Grant dollars paid teachers for release time from the classroom and visits to other schools where the kinds of practices we envisioned were already in place. Our plan was to bring together the three groups with their completed designs in March for a series of intensive sessions from which, we hoped, a master design would emerge that incorporated the best ideas from all three.

We went to work. The small groups began meeting, often at people's homes. An esprit de corps developed. Every other week the entire team would meet to update members on progress in the small groups. We also set up several visits to school sites within a day's drive. Typically, teams of three persons, one person from each small group, would travel together. We visited Thayer High School in Winchester, New Hampshire, an early member of the Coalition of Essential Schools, the Scarsdale Alternative School in New York, and Central Park East Secondary School in Manhattan. One member of the design team who was touring Germany visited the Holweide Gesamtschule in Cologne, which had recently been profiled in an article by Albert Shanker.

During this portion of our work, I began to worry that the small groups might become singularly committed to their designs and that, by March, it would be difficult to overcome their small group loyalties in the interest of a blended master plan. Nothing about anyone's personality fed this concern, only a hunch that the process itself might generate this tendency. To shift the dynamic, we decided to hold the first of our large group meetings early, in January, to review progress. We stressed the noncompetitive spirit of the work and encouraged all to freely raid each other's ideas. This meeting also served to remind us all about the approaching March deadline.

Running simultaneous to the work of the design team were the efforts of another group. We had determined in the fall that community participation and support would be essential to the project. We therefore established a community advisory group and invited our school's parent-teacher organization to select eight parents to join. We also invited the student senate to do likewise with eight students. A local banker agreed to serve as a representative from the town's chamber of commerce. We held three dinner meetings with the lab school community advisory group during the winter months. We solicited their ideas for the lab school design and asked them to critique work in progress from the small groups.

Come March, all three designs were completed and submitted on time. We gave ourselves a week to review each other's work before meeting. During this time, the designs were distributed to colleagues who were not involved in the design work but who critiqued the work for an honorarium. The critiques were circulated within the design team. We then conducted three half-day sessions to build the master design. Fortunately, we were able to obtain the services of Harold Williams, a gifted group facilitator and president of the nearby Rensselaerville Institute. Hal's skillful guidance was essential in bringing the group to consensus. We held the three meetings at five-day intervals to allow time for conversation and reflection between sessions. At the end of the third meeting, we were largely in agreement on a master design. Then, bad news arrived.

The Teachers Association and the district had been deadlocked in negotiations for a new contract to replace one that would expire in June. An impasse was declared, and the Teachers Association asked its membership to withhold all voluntary services until an agreement could be reached. We faced a dilemma: either continue our "voluntary" work to maintain momentum for the project or stop work to show solidarity with colleagues whose vote we would later seek. We chose the latter, and the work simply stopped. The many complex conversations already in progress, needed to bring the work to completion, were left hanging, incomplete. We worried about the response of our funders.

Then, in June, an agreement was reached and, suddenly, we were back in business. But it was also the end of the school year and members of the design team were scattering for the summer. During July and August, several of us stuck around to carry on the essential conversations. Through correspondence (prior to e-mail) with others, we were able to check the final recommendations with the far-flung membership and had a formal document ready for submission to faculty members and the school board by September. Our sponsors, fortunately, did not complain about the delay over the contractual dispute, and, in fact, one suggested our decision to stop work on the project was the wiser course of action.

Shortly after returning to school in September 1992, the document was distributed to all faculty and board of education members, leaders in the Teachers Association, and members of our community advisory group. We scheduled meetings with all parties to solicit questions and concerns and to consider possible changes in the document based on issues raised at these meetings. Members of the design team held a work session to make changes. During these meetings, the board indicated its readiness to unanimously approve the program should the faculty vote go favorably.

At a high school faculty meeting in October, the design team, joined by the superintendent of schools, the board president, and the Teachers Association president presented the final version. The faculty voted the following day. Seventy-five percent voted in favor of the lab school. After four years of effort, we had our school, or so we thought. More challenges lay ahead as we sought to put into practice the ideas that were dancing in our heads.

The next challenge was the recruitment of students. While the notions of a small community, individual attention to students, and project-based learning appealed to many, the absence of elective courses and a New York State Regents diploma, as well as a fear of isolation from students in the larger high school, turned many—often the same people—away. We began that first year with just fifty-one students, fewer than we had planned, which necessitated our teaching part time in the lab school and part time in the high school. The lower numbers also led some members of the high school faculty to call for another faculty vote, which was held, and which was favorable, but just barely—45 to 41. Though our first year was bumpy as we defined our school's culture internally while also developing our interface with the larger system, the school survived its infancy and has since gone on to become a regular feature of the school district, serving about 120 students in grades 9–12.

The interface with the larger system was crafted in several ways, summarized as follows:

1. No special favors: One factor that helped protect the lab school through its infancy was the pledge that resources provided to the lab school by the district would be the same as those provided to other programs. The public nature of this pledge removed considerable pressure. Whatever scrutiny

we faced from community and colleagues, we knew, at least, that it would not be resentment that, somehow, we had it easier.

2. Collaborative design: The process of developing the lab school began with an inquiry. It included a wide cross section of district personnel and members of the local community, and the design that emerged reflected the thinking of many people. The high level of collaboration and the unhurried process allowed both the forum and time for all parties involved in and affected by the process to make the emotional and intellectual adjustments necessary for the innovation to succeed. The "gears" of the larger system are not just policies and practices, they are, more fundamentally, people's beliefs and attitudes.

3. The Impact Committee: In the course of our design work, we anticipated that questions from and conflict with the larger school would, to some degree, accompany the lab school as long as it existed. Acknowledging this dynamic led us to consider jointly with skeptics whether a mechanism might be fashioned that would allow parties to address issues without an air of crisis, as a matter of the course of business. What resulted was "The Impact Committee," made up of high school and lab school representatives who met regularly, through the early years, with the high school principal. Its tough-sounding name suggested to skeptics that it meant business. Its existence, like a lightning rod, drew high-voltage attacks away from the school to neutral ground. It worked for everyone and was quite literally *the* interface between the innovation and the system. It was the doctor monitoring the transplanted organ to head off potential tissue rejection.

4. Permeable borders: Lack of communication between parties with a tense relationship is an excellent way to ensure hostility. Hostility among nations in conflict (Ireland, the Middle East, Cold War belligerents) deepens in the absence of talk and softens with communication. Lab school students mingled with high school students during lunch, in physical education classes, between classes in the hallways, and in after-school sports and clubs. High school teachers were invited to serve as jurors for the twice-yearly exhibitions that lab school students were expected to mount. Lab school teachers taught high school classes and attended high school faculty meetings. Porous borders helped maintain regular informal and formal relations and the goodwill so crucial to success.

5. College outreach: Lab school parents and students worried most about how lab schoolers would fare in the college admission process. While they felt confident that the lab school would prepare students for college academics and college life, there was a concern that the absence of a New York State Regents diploma, the institution of an alternative assessment system, and the absence of advanced placement (AP) and honors designations for course work would disadvantage lab school students applying for admission to competitive colleges.

To address these worries, we reached out to a representative sample of colleges and universities—likely options for our graduates—even before the school opened. We needed to persuade colleges that this alternative school was academically serious and not flaky, and that the absence of a Regents diploma allowed for a more focused curriculum, emphasizing depth of understanding as opposed to some sort of easy way out. It turned out that the lab school was a relatively easy sell. Once colleges understood what we were about, they embraced the qualities that our students promised to bring to their classes and campus life. The outreach was crucial in clearing this hurdle. It created the interface that helped make the innovation work.

Larger Lessons

How do we effectively support promising innovation? How do we keep the larger system from crushing it? How do we create workable interfaces between the two? How do we promote innovations on their merits rather than simply on their fit? The three scenarios that follow suggest strategies at three levels of the system: the classroom, the faculty room, and the boardroom.

Classroom Encounters

"Can you please just tell us the answer?!," a plaintive student in the third row wants to know. What she wants to know is the information that will be on the test. What you insistently are doing is withholding "answers" and teaching your students to think their way through their own conclusions. This particular student is smart enough to realize that the modes of thinking associated with your inquiry approach to instruction will not be featured on the test. She is also smart enough to know that "the test," devised by the state Department of Education in response to NCLB, is what counts. The gears of the larger system are calibrated to the dispensing of facts. The gears of teaching and learning in your classroom are calibrated to habits of inquiry and reflection. Your student is reminding you that, as wonderful as you may think you are as a teacher, you're not giving your students what they need to survive in the system.

Talk about a moral dilemma! How do you do what you know is right in your classroom when all around you the system's gears demand that you comply with bad educational practice or get shredded to pieces. You are caught in the Grand Interlock, the tendency of schools to spread conformity and crush promising innovation. Got something new to introduce? Its acceptance by the system will be determined not by its value for learning but mainly by its fit.

And yet, there is always something you can do. What the system demands and what you know to be good teaching and learning are not wholly separate.

The system demands factual/conceptual information. You know that good teaching and learning are about inquiry, analysis, reflection, and the social construction of knowledge. These two realms, as much as they represent epistemologically different starting points, do overlap. You need to focus your inquiry on *something* in the world, to analyze and reflect upon *some* matter of substance, and your students' new knowledge will be constructed from *some* experientially based building blocks of reality. There are facts and concepts galore in that mix. There is also a surfeit of inquiry and reflection. Therefore, you need to be in the habit of asking, what do my students need to know for the test, and how can I incorporate that information into lessons grounded in sound pedagogy? This is a question that keeps one eye on the demands of the system and the other on the demands of good teaching. It is, in the context of your classroom, the workable interface that you construct on a daily basis.

The dual focus that you need to maintain extends beyond matters of curriculum. You can apply it to almost any area of daily practice as a teacher. For example, the system promotes professional isolation through its regimentation of instruction into subjects, periods, and classrooms with a single teacher as well as its objectification of teachers as interchangeable parts that may be inserted here or there as the machine requires. In contrast, you know that good teaching is nurtured through collaboration with other teachers who examine their instructional efforts together and analyze student work to inform their ongoing practice. In almost any school you will be able to find like-minded colleagues who share your values, who are willing to consider some level of collaboration, and who in fact, like you, crave it in order to maintain their ability to do good work. Carve out your own times and places to look together at student work, to examine each other's lessons and assessments. Good teachers have always done this at the margins of our mechanized system of schooling. And it is always possible, just maybe, that if enough teachers in your school become engaged in collaborative efforts on their own, you will be able to make a case with the powers that be in your locality to alter the system ever so slightly to support such work. One way to change the system is to push back against it with the moral force of large numbers of people striving to do the right thing in spite of what the system dictates. Such is the story of the American civil rights movement. Eventually the system relented against the moral force of thousands of committed individuals who began simply to act upon the dictates of their conscience. There is, indeed, power in collective action, which leads us to the section just ahead.

Teacher Talk

Imagine you've had a brainstorm of an idea. It solves multiple problems and is easy to implement. You work it all out in your head, and then you present it enthusiastically to your colleagues. You anticipate excited interest, skeptics turned toward the light of your brilliant solution, a nod of approval, even from the veteran curmudgeon. Instead you are met with the following:

"We tried that already. It didn't work."
"They won't let us do that."
"It might have worked *there*, but *our* kids are different."
"Sure. If they give us more funding, which they'll never do, we
    can make it happen."

Your heart starts to break as these comments are followed up with stories of similarly exciting plans that crashed on the rocky shoreline of an entrenched system. You are not buoyed when, as a final comment, one colleague offers patronizingly, "But that's good. You keep having ideas like that and maybe you'll come up with something." You walk away knowing that whatever idea you come up with next will be sure to sink like a rock with this group!

Though disheartening, the response of your colleagues is understandable. Anyone who has worked in a school through one cycle of "reform" (roughly equal to one and a half times the tenure of the most recent superintendent) has learned how the system rejects change. Those of us who have lived through multiple cycles of "reform" can begin to predict where the system will bear down on innovation, exactly where the gears will grind. But to stop there and conclude that the system will never change, and that innovation is impossible, is to quit too soon.

"We tried that, it didn't work" merits some picking apart. "We" who? How hard did "we" actually "try"? What is "that"? And what "didn't work" about it? If you could engage one of your colleagues in a thoughtful conversation around those questions, you both would most certainly gain insight into the change process. If past attempts at change are not simply deployed to dump water on the fire of innovation but examined as lessons in how to stoke a flame that will be sustained, then your brilliant idea might actually stand a chance.

Asking such questions begins the process of change. Dismissive statements, such as the aforementioned, are used as a kind of armor to deflect efforts to initiate change. Since change in schools has so often meant painful emotional experiences that have gone nowhere, many conclude that it is better to avoid getting excited, yet again, about possibilities that have grown dim than to get battered, yet again, by the system. "Been there, done that" covers any innovation you are likely to conjure and allows whomever chooses to utter it the easy path of rejecting something without ever having considered it. Asking that very colleague, in fact, where she or he has been and what she or he has done begins to push beneath the surface of a throwaway comment, even as it honors the experience of a veteran colleague.

In *Pedagogy of the Oppressed*, Brazilian educator Paulo Freire explains that the ultimate oppression is the internalization of oppression by the oppressed. He writes, "The oppressed, having internalized the image of the oppressor and adopted his guidelines, are fearful of freedom. Freedom would require them to eject this image and replace it with autonomy and responsibility."[2] The path out of oppression, Freire continues, is not for the oppressed to overpower their oppressor and take over but, rather, to liberate both oppressor and oppressed from the mentality of domination that controls both.

Though our circumstances are far different from those of the Brazilian peasants about whom Freire wrote, in a similar way we as educators have internalized the gears of the system, which dictate that schools operate in a certain way. Well before an innovation meets up with the system, it meets up with the image of the system that operates in our heads. We have become the system. "We tried that, it didn't work." Transformation of schools begins with our liberation from the mentality of the system. Engaging each other critically in conversation about past efforts is one way that conversation begins.

Public Engagement

"No AP courses?"
"No electives?"
"No grades?"
"No rankings?"
"How will they do on the (fill-in-the-blank state) tests?"
"Will they be prepared for the SAT?"
"How are they going to get into college?"

High school is shaped by the perceived demands of college. Middle school is shaped by the perceived demands of high school. Elementary school is shaped by the perceived demands of middle school. And so it goes. It is no wonder, then, that as you face a group of parents at an information session about the new "progressive" alternative school under development in your district, the concerns that surface have nothing to do with learning per se and everything to do with the attainment structure of the system. For selective colleges, the criteria for selection include AP courses, challenging electives, grades, rankings, and test scores. Just as the outside pressure of curriculum frameworks enforces conformity in the classroom, so the outside pressure of college admission enforces conformity in the structure and expectations of the school as a whole.

What if the pressure of college admission were removed and schools were free to reinvent secondary education around goals of student growth and learning unalloyed by the requirements of college admission? What would school begin to look like? We have reason to believe that it would begin to look subtly and importantly different because of an experiment that was conducted in the 1930s.

In 1933, the Progressive Education Association obtained consent from leading colleges and universities to waive the usual high school graduation requirements for a select cohort of high schools involved in a unique study. The purpose of the study was to see what sorts of innovations would flower in high schools freed from college admission requirements while being held to high expectations for student learning—to be defined locally and collaboratively. What resulted from The Eight-Year Study (1933–1941) was indeed a flowering of innovative practices and documented achievement across a range of indicators of academic and civic knowledge and habits. Findings from the study, released in late 1941, showed signs of moving American secondary education toward a tipping point that might have resulted in wide-ranging changes.[3] Then Pearl Harbor was attacked by the Japanese in early December, Congress declared war, and the nation suddenly had other, more pressing priorities. When the war was over, a conservative mood prevailed, and the potential learning from The Eight-Year Study was lost. A follow-up study of the thirty schools in the original cohort, conducted in 1952, found that without the support of the Progressive Education Association and the commitment by colleges to waive their customary admission requirements, all of the high schools involved had returned to their former state of subservience to the larger system.[4]

The lesson might appear to be that the system is just too large, and that isolated attempts stand no chance. But here is an alternative lesson: the thirty schools in the study cohort moved forward by virtue of an agreement with a number of colleges who were persuaded of the potential value of the Progressive Education Association's experiment. What is to keep an individual school with similar progressive ambitions from cultivating relationships with colleges and universities to which its graduates are likely to seek admission? Indeed, it can be done. In the cases of both the Bethlehem Lab School and the Parker Charter School (profiled in chapter 3), that is exactly what happened. Careful and personal outreach by leaders in each school to a number of colleges and universities raised awareness of and respect for the alternative path to a rigorous education that each school represented. College admission representatives were invited to work with both schools in designing alternative transcripts and other credentials that students would submit. When graduates from both schools sent in their applications, the admissions offices were ready and eager to review them. They knew that these were serious schools with a genuine focus on student learning and engagement. Over the years, word spread to other colleges, and as graduates applied to different schools, there was already a track record that could be shared with those colleges attesting to the success of graduates from both schools.

But back to the scenario just described: before launching the parent meeting, do some homework. Find examples of other schools that have forged a similar path and that have a track record of college success for their graduates.

Make some inquiries yourself to those colleges to get the ball rolling. *Then* meet with the parents, acknowledge their concerns, show them the persuasive evidence that alternative approaches *can* succeed, and explain that outreach has already begun on behalf of your school district's initiative.

Countering the Culture

1. Innovation *is* possible. The five cases featured in this book are persuasive evidence that the interfaces necessary to sustain change through the medium and long term can be crafted in the real world of American schooling. What is required is the persistence to see past the initial barriers and to maintain a dual focus on the innovation itself, as well as the procedural, political, and cultural adjustments necessary to sustain it.

2. The system *can* change. Historian Michael Katz has written about the development of our contemporary system of public schools. He shows how in the full tide of the nineteenth century there were several possible directions in which the system could have moved and how the actions of groups of people moved it in a particular direction.[5] Likewise, historians David Tyack and Larry Cuban also show, by drawing persuasively on the historical record, that systemic change *is* possible. In *Tinkering toward Utopia*, they point out that opportunities for change arise periodically and will sometimes persist if embodied in legislation, or if they produce "influential constituencies" that lobby for their continuation.[6] As innovators, it is our job to be watchful for these opportunities. They may be local (a new industry in town that increases the property tax revenues) or more remote (a new state law), but they appear, and we need to be on the lookout for them and ready to act.

3. Even when the system isn't changing, there are often strong countercurrents that will support innovation in the eddies. For example, even though the dominant ethos of schools is the industrial mind-set, there has always been a progressive impulse to support progressive-minded educators and families who create spaces for themselves at the margins of the system. Sometimes these marginal efforts can push back against the mainstream and alter its flow.

4. We have internalized the gears of the system and must transform ourselves to imagine different possibilities if we are to transform the system. Systemic change begins with personal change.

Case Closed

The Bethlehem Lab School is a program that came into existence in a particular place at a particular time. The events, personalities, opportunities, and challenges it faced on the path to its eventual success are unique. In considering similar initiatives elsewhere, one could justifiably and unconstructively assert, "We tried that, it didn't work." Or, "It worked there because they, . . . but it won't work here because we . . ." Alternatively, one can ask, what are the opportunities in my school setting? What are the barriers? Where can I find a space among the spinning gears of the larger system where a different microsystem can be established? How can I build a workable interface with the larger system? How can I, in collaboration with others, push back against the system and gather the momentum that would bring about systemic change? Can it be done? It can. People do it all the time.

5

The Politics of Appeasement

Framing the Issue

I don't like to disappoint people. My guess is, you don't either. Teaching and learning are about relationships, and many of us went into education because we understand and value constructive human relations. We don't like to disappoint our students, or their parents. We don't like to disappoint our supervisors. When asked to do something legitimate, our cheery inclination is to say yes, to accommodate, to do what we can.

> Could you please speak with my daughter about her writing? She seems discouraged lately.
>
> Would you mind teaching the ninth-grade math course next year? We really need someone who's an excellent instructor. We need you.
>
> Is there some way we can address the bullying problem?
>
> Can you provide some challenge activities for the students who are ready?
>
> Can I ask you to look at math assessment practices in your building?
>
> There's a demand for more foreign languages. Can we look into offering French?
>
> Can we add more electives? More APs?
>
> The state tests are covering a wider range of topics. We need to adjust.
>
> Our sports program needs more offerings. What can we do about that?
>
> We need a second late-bus run. Can you figure it out?
>
> How about a lunchtime detention system?

If we say yes to every defensible request, and we try to do *all* things, then pretty soon we do nothing well. If our filter for decision making is how loud or insistent or logical or influential the voices for change are, without

93

consideration of the school's essential mission, then the outcome is appeasement, not improvement. Pretty soon our ship of education is rudderless and adrift in a swirling tide—with lots of rocky shoreline and sandbars awash in rolling surf nearby. What do we do? Do we *just say no*? How do we know when to say yes? Or maybe? Where do we draw the line? What line? Is line drawing the right way to think about it? What are the right questions to ask our suitors as they petition us? How do we decide? The cost of decisions driven by the desire to appease is high, as the case in point for this chapter bears witness. Balancing our desire to please with a desire to protect the essential mission of our school is crucial, ultimately, to the success of our students. In the Beaver Country Day School (BCDS), this chapter's "case in point," we see a fine example of a school that managed for nearly two decades to resist the politics of appeasement by remaining true to its original vision. In doing so, it was able to serve its students well with purposeful and focused attention. It lived out the aphorism made popular decades later by Ted Sizer, that "less is more." Its energetic commitment to its founding vision offers a lesson to educators anywhere, and its drift from that vision in the 1940s serves, like the demise of the Temple School, as a cautionary tale. Unlike the Temple School, however, the Beaver Country Day School did not go quietly into that good night. It found its bearings, reasserted its original vision and mission, and transformed itself into the vibrant center of progressive pedagogy that it is today.

Case in Point

The Beaver Country Day School began as an effort by several prominent Boston families to provide continued schooling for children, including their own, who were then enrolled in a small, private kindergarten and primary school located at 9 Beaver Place in Boston. The children were growing older, and their parents worried that the offerings of Boston's private schools of the day would be too rigid for their taste. Might the little school on Beaver Place be expanded beyond its current third-grade class, they wondered? The idea found support among other parents, and to help forward the emerging project, the group invited Eugene Randolph Smith of Baltimore, a prominent progressive educator of the day, to give a talk at the home of one of the parent leaders. To have attracted a figure of such prominence to speak in such an intimate venue underscores the relative social influence of the families involved.

After Smith's visit in April 1920, the idea took off. A headline in the *Boston Evening Transcript* from February 1921 announced, "Another Country Day School for Boston,"[1] and the new school, which soon found a home in the fashionable Chestnut Hill neighborhood, commenced its first term that year with a plan to enroll students from grade four through high school graduation.[2]

From its inception, the Beaver Country Day School reflected thoughtful pedagogical ideals. In the historical moment of Beaver's founding, the torchbearer of those ideals was the progressive education movement. As one of its leading exponents, Eugene Randolph Smith was successfully wooed by the Beaver parents to leave his post as head of the famous Park School in Baltimore to lead their new venture in Chestnut Hill, just three miles west of Boston but just far enough from the urban scene to earn its "country day school" designation.

As an educator, Smith stands squarely in the liberal tradition with Rousseau, Froebel, Alcott, and Parker. Yet his work also signals the "modern" twentieth-century ideas that progressivism packed around the ideological core of its liberal forebears. His speech that April evening in 1920 extolled the genius of children, the importance of free play, and the role of the teacher, not as imparter of knowledge but as facilitator of learning.[3] His speech also invokes the new (at that time) application of standardized tests to measure intelligence, as well as other "scientific" advances to guide instruction and assessment. Early literature from the school also shows this blending of a thoughtful instructional approach with an emerging science of education. The prospectus of BCDS from 1923 reads like a page torn from John Dewey's journal: "The teachers will guide and use the interests and impulses of childhood rather than repress them. Much of the work will be founded on the pupils' real or imaginary participation in each situation, rather than on an assignment of rote lesson to be subsequently heard in formal recitations."[4]

At the same time that the school amply displayed its Deweyan ideals, it also put into practice progressivism's commitment to the new science. The same brochure proclaims: "It has been conclusively proved that the unguided opinions of teachers as to the progress of their pupils are very inaccurate. The Beaver Country Day School will therefore check the opinions of its teachers by the use of standardized tests which have been given to many thousands of schoolchildren."[5] Though standardized tests were applied, including IQ tests, the Beaver Country Day School prided itself on the fact that selection was not based on IQ test results. Promotional literature from this early period boasts that Beaver "is one of the few schools which is trying to educate girls of varying abilities."[6]

Beaver quickly cemented a favorable reputation as a progressive school. An internal document entitled, "Professional Activities of the Beaver Country Day School, during the First Half Year, 1924–1925," talks about many visitors from as far away as India and Belgium. It notes also that the headmaster had been invited to give summer courses at Harvard and New York State Normal College, and that he had lectured at many civic and educational organizations around the country.[7] From the same era, an article in the *Cambridge Tribune* reads, "A rather unique educational enterprise, prospering wonderfully . . . hopes to make a substantial contribution to education by reason of the greater latitude of its training, and closer attention to the well rounded development of a child than is possible in the more rigid public school system."[8] To some degree, the new school was also intended as a demonstration site, a kind of laboratory for the dissemination of progressive practices. A group of Beaver teachers who in the early 1940s authored a history of the school, write that the founders "thought there was a need in that locality for a demonstration school of a progressive 'Country Day School' type."[9] Interestingly, the same volume also points out that as part of its "demonstration" role, the Beaver Country Day School established a teacher training program with "16 to 25 college graduates in its apprentice group each year."[10] For a school of such small size, so many teacher trainees must have brought enormous relief to the school's operating budget while driving average class size to enviably low numbers. It is interesting to note as an aside that this is the same strategy used by Francis Parker in Quincy to reduce class size there in the 1870s. This document also identifies homerooms with typically twenty students and subject classes with twenty "or fewer." Small classes no doubt furthered the goals of thoughtfully individualizing learning.

In 1932, when the Progressive Education Association embarked on what became the landmark Eight-Year Study, Beaver was well positioned to play a role. As an already prominent progressive school, it quickly rose to the top in a careful selection of 30 schools out of 250 that were nominated to participate in the study. As the study got under way, participation stimulated the Beaver faculty to more deeply and energetically embrace its progressive pedagogical ideals as well as push students hard to higher levels of achievement. Successive reports from the Eight-Year Study heralded Beaver as being particularly noteworthy for its student achievement, and the final reports measuring success in college showed Beaver graduates performing exceptionally well.[11]

From its inception through the 1930s, the Beaver Country Day School hewed closely to its original mission; however, shortly after the Eight-Year Study concluded, a combination of internal and external events tugged Beaver away from its pedagogical center and nearly wiped out the school. Though the school was able to survive the depression years financially, the war years seem to have hit it hard. By 1945, it was near bankruptcy, with declining enrollments and imminent foreclosure on a $262,000 mortgage. At the very brink of the abyss, Beaver parents and alumni stepped in and raised enough money to refinance the school's mortgage and set it back onto a viable, though still shaky, course. Because of the school's prominence, its near demise caught the eye of *Time* magazine editors, who offer an interesting analysis in the December 24, 1945, issue. The entire article reads as follows:

Like Beavers [headline]
The Beaver Country Day School was founded when John Dewey's ideas on progressive education were rearing their bumptious little

heads. "Education generally was a pretty stale dish," recalls its headmaster. "Green mold is not limited to penicillin. Many a school has flourished in mold and called it tradition."

Beaver School for girls, started in a stable on Boston's proud Beacon Hill, now inhabits a million-dollar home in suburban Brookline. Not quite so "progressive" as it once was, Beaver draws a set of well-heeled bobby-soxers (42 of Boston's current crop of 130 debs are Beaver girls) and succeeds pretty well in making scholars of them. But Beaver only paid off $10,000 of its $262,000 original mortgage. Last month, a Boston bank, tired of the green mold forming around Beaver's I.O.U.s, threatened to foreclose. One alumna dumped her four children in the back of the car [and] made the rounds of friends to solicit funds.

Last week, Beaver girls, past and present, gathered to celebrate the 25th anniversary of the school's charter and to learn whether there would be [a] 26th. There would be. Working like their namesakes, loyal Beavers had saved their school by raising $105,000 in three weeks.[12]

In chronicling the school's near financial demise, the *Time* article also hints at cracks in the school's pedagogical foundation. This is confirmed in research by Frederick Redefer of the schools of the Eight-Year Study in a doctoral dissertation at Teachers College, Columbia University, completed eight years after the original study ended. Reviewing the state of each school, Redefer found that among the subject schools in general and at one school (likely Beaver) in particular, most of the progressive pedagogical gains had been lost. The school, he writes, "in the words of the present headmaster, has the same drive but with mastery of skills and acquisition of facts stressed. Or, as one faculty member reported, the school now has greater efficiency in meeting college requirements."[13]

It is hard to say no to requests that, on their face, are reasonable, particularly if you need the support of whomever is making the request. Schools are inevitably beholden to their parent-clients whether directly, as with an independent school or a public school of choice, where parents may elect to leave, or, obliquely, in a district school, where parents influence board policy and can make life agreeable or miserable for teachers and school administrators by vocally expressing their delight or dismay.

The Beaver Country Day School enjoyed over two decades of focused commitment to a compelling and simple vision. Surely during that period there were those who petitioned for changes that may have sounded reasonable—a somewhat more traditional approach to classroom subjects perhaps, or less time devoted to superfluous "arts and crafts." Compromises could have been made. A small course change here, a slight adjustment of emphasis there. And, gradually, the essence of a thoughtfully focused school would be lost. But the school held true to its vision and resisted such reasonable entreaties in the interest of a defined purpose. However, that began to change in the late 1930s, when financial realities pressured school leaders to oblige the requests for a little change here and there.

The record suggests that financial pressures began to build in the late 1930s, even as the school was enjoying a grand reputation enhanced by its prominence in the Eight-Year Study. Board minutes and correspondence from 1938 suggest growing debt. Board members worried openly about the conflict between a plan to build an endowment at a time when the school was apparently exposed to considerable unsecured debt.[14] Matters worsened over the next few years. One archival document from the mid-1940s[15] reads:

> The record through 1941 was fairly satisfactory, but during the three-year period from August 1, 1941, to June 30, 1944, the school lost in operations $46,649 in cash, wiping out its working capital and producing a deficiency.

A report from Treasurer Elbert A. Harvey, dated February 11, 1947, confirms what *Time* magazine reported: "In November 1945 Beaver was threatened with foreclosure of a $252,500 mortgage on all of its buildings and developments and on ten of its 15 acres of land."[16]

The school recognized its vulnerability and began to adjust its planning accordingly in order to remain financially viable—and in so doing it began to lose its course philosophically. One record from the period offers:

> The future well-being of the Beaver Country Day School seems to me to depend more upon a good enrollment of the best types of pupil than upon endowment. Without the former, the latter would be of no avail.[17]

Such declarations are a far cry from the principled commitment at the school's inception that it was to be "one of the few schools that is trying to educate girls of varying abilities."[18]

The commentary continues: "Our enrollment below the Senior High School could be improved, and its quality also bettered. To my mind, the principal reasons for this are, first, a lack of the right community relations (due to personal qualities in the managers of the school itself) and, second, hard times."[19]

Mission drift continued through the 1940s. The February 24, 1943, "Clearinghouse Committee" minutes read, "The chairman then introduced Mrs. Gerould, the new "Field Secretary," who gave an interesting talk on her conception of a Public Relations Program for the Beaver School. With the ultimate aim of an improved enrollment, she touched on the importance of the total picture or impression that the school makes on the public."[20]

This total picture, according to subsequent archival material from the same era, is striking. Trustees were apparently considering radically different and very tradition-bound ideas. Notes from a speech by John Mahoney of Boston University about civic education, included among various meeting minutes, include the comment, "We must have a citizenry that is more law-abiding."[21] A Boston University test is cited, showing how few adults know the following names: "Sidney Hillman (secretary of the Treasury), Tom Connolly (Archbishop of Boston), and Bilbo (a musician)." This swing toward what in a later time would be called cultural literacy represents a radically different impulse from the founding spirit of the school and a clear gesture toward "the impression that the school makes on the public."

Larger Lessons

The politics of appeasement, like all politics, represents trade-offs. Take a position and you will fail to attract certain members of the polis. Hold your ground when the going gets tough and you will alienate still more. Move off your center a bit, call it flexibility, and you gain some back but lose others. Move further still and you are seen as spineless—a flip-flopper. Soon everybody walks away. This essential dynamic gets played out in various ways in education all the time. The story of the Beaver Country Day School is one example. What goes on in our classrooms, our faculty rooms, and in our work with the public provides many more.

Classroom Encounters

"I can't imagine leaving out the ecology unit. That would be irresponsible. I could trim back the structure of the cell unit a bit, but then my students won't have the foundation they need for the unit on mitosis. I know: I'll cut out organic chemistry. Just leave it out. Of course, that would mean I'd need to do some extra teaching for the chemistry behind the respiration unit. What I really need is an extra month to teach my biology course!"

As teachers, we love our chosen subject almost as much as we love our students. We want others to experience the power of our disciplines to explain the world in just the way we have experienced it. We want to share our wonder for the universe as it unfolds through the lense of biology or history or mathematics or the arts or literature, and so on. Understandably, we want to teach it all, but we know that we can't. Thus the politics of appeasement, as it plays itself out in classroom practice, is often an interior monologue. It is the voice inside us that wishes to be appeased. It is our own love for the discipline we teach that threatens to smother itself. It is *all* important. We can't leave *anything* out.

In this respect, the difference between the Beaver Country Day School example and the snippet of interior monologue above is one of scale only. Both are about the necessity of judicious restraint. Both must rely on a clear understanding of what the work is most essentially about in order to make responsible choices about how to proceed. For the Beaver Country Day School, it was about a clear understanding of the school's institutional mission, mined from its founding documents. For any teacher battling the voices in her or his own head, it is about the essential objectives for a course of study. What do you want your students to know and be able to do?

Grant Wiggins and Jay McTighe, in *Understanding by Design*, offer a thoughtful path through this dilemma.[22] Based on decades of work devoted to curriculum design issues, Wiggins and McTighe suggest a conceptualization of curriculum as three concentric circles. In the outermost ring goes all the information that one might become familiar with in studying a topic. In the second ring are knowledge and skills instrumental to a topic. In the innermost ring are placed enduring understandings, knowledge that is essential to the topic, understandings that will take root and endure beyond the unit test or final essay or lab write-up and become foundational to the learner's growing repertoire of knowledge with which to mediate experience.[23] When the voice inside our head tells us it is *all* important, Wiggins and McTighe's concepction of curriculum is a useful guide for doing what we know we must but find so difficult. It helps us separate the merely important from the truly essential and rather than simplistically suggesting that a line be drawn for which some gets included and some gets excluded, it allows us to include much but to structure curriculum appropriately to give central attention to central understandings and peripheral attention to peripheral information. For the science teacher pondering which units to cut, it provides the opportunity to prioritize essential knowledge that crosses units of study, thus providing a framework in which to place a trimmer and more meaningful selection of key concepts and skills.

Teacher Talk

Negotiation for a new teachers' contract has not been going well. The old contract expired in June, and it is now December. The union membership has voted for work to rule. All professional teacher activity beyond duties out-lined in the contract must cease. Thus the pressure of collective action will be brought to bear in order to break the negotiation impasse. You assess the work you are currently doing to see what's voluntary: your after-school, extra-help sessions, your participation in the district's School Reform Committee, your monthly "lesson study" meetings with several colleagues interested in examining teaching practice together, the action research project you were invited by your superintendent to participate in through the nearby state university, your daily arrival at school a good hour before the contract stipulates, and your frequent lingering in the afternoon, sometimes two hours beyond dismissal time. Among these voluntary commitments are many persons and groups whom you might feel the need to "appease" in the face of the contract crisis: students, parents, supervisors, colleagues, union stalwarts. But saying yes to everyone in this instance seems impossible if you value your integrity. Deception would be inevitable if you indulged your customary desire to give a big cheery yes to all legitimate requests. And, indeed, all of the requests implied in the union move, and the voluntary activities have a legitimate basis. How do you proceed? Not with a policy of appeasement. Simply saying yes, merely indulging your wish to maintain cheery relations, is to value your own integrity less than a smooth surface. But how do you decide what to do, and what do you say to those you will inevitably disappoint?

No one can tell you what you should do, but there are questions you can ask yourself that will prompt a more thoughtful series of choices. These questions are not unlike those an institution asks itself when faced with multiple, conflicting requests, and they are not unlike those you ask yourself about the development of curriculum when it *all* seems so important. Ask yourself, what is most important? Then ask, what is also important, but not quite as much? Then ask, what is actually less important? Then, analogous to Wiggins and McTighe's concentric circles, ask how you can pay some appropriate attention to the less important while giving your most attention to what is essential. So, for example, you might reason in this way. Serving my students well is most important. Supporting the collective action of the union is also important, but not quite as much. Serving my own professional development is important, too, but if I have to prioritize, I'll put it, at the moment at least, beneath the other two. Next, rather than drawing a sharp line that rules in certain activities and rules out others, think in terms of concentric circles and ask, how can I serve my priorities with the level of attention that each deserves? Since serving your students is central, but respecting your union's efforts is also important, is there a way you can make some adjustments to respect both? Might you curtail your after-school sessions but still offer to meet with students most in need during the fifteen minutes before homeroom when you are required to be in school? It is less time, but taking advantage of it sends a message to your students that you are trying to find a way, even in difficult circumstances, to attend to their needs. In weighing the lesser but still important value of your own professional development, might you temporarily suspend the action research project, since, by its nature, it can be easily picked up again once the contract is settled? Then there's your lesson study group. You find this deeply rewarding and restorative. You hate to miss these meetings, but might you decide with your group to engage in a somewhat simplified protocol over e-mail that keeps you in touch with each other's practice and provides helpful feedback without the long meetings, just until the contract is settled? Then there's the School Reform Committee. Perhaps this simply has to stop. It is a clearly public expression of voluntarism, it is directly engaged with the district with whom the negotiations have stalled, and the impact on your students of ceasing this activity is pretty close to zero.

So far, you've taken a principled approach to your actions. To you, it feels honest and fair and true to your priorities. But what do you say to everyone it might impact?

Here again, no one can tell you what to say. But there are some questions to ask yourself to help you sort it out. Where is there likely to be misunderstanding if you say nothing? Why does it matter for someone to know or not know the motive for your actions? Where there is likely to be misunderstanding, and where that misunderstanding could be consequential, is where you need to speak up. For example, making a general announcement in the faculty room about your oh-so-thoughtful decisions about how to proceed heroically through the work-to-rule order would be simple grandstanding. On the other hand, the parent of a student with whom you have been working, who calls you to ask how the after-school sessions are going, merits a more thoughtful response. Most likely, the superintendent's office will not need a complicated explanation as to why you will not be attending the next School Reform Committee meeting. The Union leadership probably has already discussed it with the district and the meeting will be cancelled anyway.

Making constructive decisions that are true to your values and your role in the organization is hard work. It sometimes goes against the impulse to please others, most of whom you like, which can momentarily disturb the calm waters of your work relationships. But being clear in what you are doing, and making your reasoning clear to those who need to understand it, is the best path to an untroubled conscience and long-term respect among those who know you. It represents the difference between appeasement and principled affirmation. Appeasement means pacifying others and possibly compromising your integrity by saying different things to different people. Principled affirmation, in contrast, is the practice of determining what you owe to different groups and being transparent in your decisions.

Public Engagement

You are the headmaster of your district's new humanities high school, one of several themed high schools that has replaced the single, comprehensive school serving the entire district. Your superintendent has given headmasters a high degree of autonomy in crafting each school's curriculum and programs. Your school's mission includes integration of the arts into the academic program. For the last two years, this has been accomplished through an interdisciplinary humanities course that weaves together history, literature, and the performing and fine arts. Students learn the fundamentals of music, fine arts, theatre, and dance as part of the program, including practical experiences with each artistic medium. Meanwhile, performance groups meet after school. A band, chorus, and small orchestra meet on different days of the week. For the most part, this has worked well in keeping the school schedule uncomplicated and flexible while allowing performance opportunities for students who sing and play musical instruments. Recently, however, there has been talk about problems associated with the music performance groups meeting after school—they conflict with sports schedules and family obligations. Some students have after-school jobs. You have received a number of inquiries regarding whether the music groups might be built into the schedule "like most other schools." Some of these inquiries have indicated that as a school of the arts and humanities, music really ought to be central to the schedule and "integrated" into the school day.

You understand these concerns *and* you want to protect the mission of the school. You worry about the impact that music groups scheduled into the day would have on the flexibility of the schedule. The simple schedule your school presently uses has been immensely helpful in allowing your teachers to craft units of study that constructively alter class configurations and the length of periods, allowing for adventures outside of the school. Adding performance groups that include only some of the students into the schedule will lock the schedule into place. What do you do? The challenge is similar in its dynamics to the other examples featured in this chapter, including the Beaver Country Day School. As with the others, the challenge is to see beneath the politics of pleasing this or that group and instead to ground your thinking, conversation, and decision making in the organization's mission. The question to ask is, what will best serve students given the mission of this school? As with the other examples in this chapter, no one can tell you the answer, but asking the right questions will steer you toward a constructive outcome. A good course of action can begin with listening carefully to those who are raising concerns. Invite these parents to speak with you at length. Ask probing questions about their concerns and their wishes. Solving a problem begins with understanding what the problem really is. It may not be a philosophical issue but only a practical one, or the reverse, or some combination. You won't know unless you really listen. You may also need to educate. Some of your petitioners may not be aware of the arts integration approach the school is using. Some may not be aware that introducing special classes into the school day would mean less opportunity for teachers to design the creative and engaging units of study that so many parents have praised the school for.

Finally, you will want to ground the conversation in what this particular school is about and how it can best serve its students. If its goal is to train young artists and performers in a particular medium of expression, then the outcome will be different than a school whose mission is to expose all students to the various forms of artistic expression and weave them together in a context of the humanities.

Years ago, Roger Fisher and William Ury of the Harvard Negotiation Project wrote a book about the art of negotiation that has become a classic in the field. The central idea of *Getting to Yes* is highly relevant to the work we do as educators.[24] Ury and Fisher remind us repeatedly in their book to focus on *interests,* not *positions.* For example, your parent petitioners have come to you with a position: "We want band during period 5." If you focus on their position, then the conversation is likely to be short and nasty. But if you ask them why they want band during period 5, you may learn that their interest lies in avoiding a scheduling conflict between band and soccer practice, in which case the solution might be as simple as shifting band practice to Wednesday, your school's early release day, thus ensuring that band students will be finished with practice before district-wide soccer practice begins. Getting at underlying interests and goals begins with careful listening, and listening begins with a genuine invitation to your public to say what's on their minds, to ask interested, probing questions, and to start a real conversation in the service of children.

Countering the Culture

Several themes run through all of the examples in this chapter. The overarching understanding is that decisions driven by a desire to please will sink the ship. Decisions driven by a thoughtful, nonideological faithfulness to institutional mission and professional role, while occasionally disturbing the surface calm of interpersonal relations, will lead in the medium and long term to far more constructive outcomes.

Some important ideas to keep in mind follow:

1. Be clear about your institutional mission and your professional role. These are your anchors that will simultaneously allow your ship to move about to accommodate shifting needs and wishes yet keep it from drifting to the rocks and shoals of pleasing people just for the sake of pleasing them.

2. Don't think about drawing a line between what you can and can't do. Instead, think of your priorities in concentric circles. What is essential, what is instrumental, and what is peripheral? Often instrumental or peripheral goals can continue to receive some attention when they are understood for the subservient role they play.

3. Listen carefully to the requests and concerns that come your way—whether they come from inside your own head or from other people. Discern the deeper issues and interests beneath the surface goals and gripes. Address the interests, not the positions.

Case Closed

By the early 1950s, the Beaver Country Day School bore almost no resemblance to its original, thoughtful self. Appeasing so many powerful petitioners in a context of financial difficulty eroded the sharp edges that had marked the school.

Nonetheless, Redefer's depressing analysis of 1952 ends with the hopeful comment, "There are indications that the school is again interested in experimentation."[25] Those indications, noted by an astute observer in 1952, grew slowly into a driving force in the following decades. By re-embracing its original institutional mission, the school began to restore its reputation as a proud progressive school. By 2000, head of school Peter Hutton was able to confidently assert, "Our peers across the country recognize us as one of a handful of schools serving as incubators of progressive education."[26] As the school's reputation was restored, so too were its enrollments. Head of school Hutton again remarks:

> The number of applicants to Beaver has risen dramatically since 1996; consequently, admission to the School has become considerably more competitive. While total enrollment has increased 25%, our acceptance rate has fallen from 75% to 57%, and our yield (the percentage of accepted students who choose Beaver) has risen from 40% to 48%.
>
> Our institutional commitment to diversity has moved us into a position where our faculty and staff population reflects exactly the rich diversity of our student population (18% people of color)—an extraordinary achievement for an independent school.[27]

The desire to please is strong, and the politics of appeasement is ultimately a counterproductive approach to professional and institutional decision making. Dare to occasionally disturb the calm surface of interpersonal relations and you will ultimately serve well your profession, your institution, and your students.

6

The Failure of Generosity and Justice

Framing the Issue

We take care of our own. It is a natural impulse, coded into our genes for the protection of our young and the preservation of our species. Who can fault a parent for wanting what is best for his or her child? No one can. In the private realm of families, this makes perfect sense. But what about the public realm of a democracy? In a democracy, who are "our own"? Who are "our young" to be protected? The answer, of course, is that "our own" and "our young" are *all* children. For the education of each and every child of this collective *we* ought to evoke a social impulse for the nurturance and protection that is as strong as the demands of our genetic code for the nurturance and protection of our own children.

Such is not the case, however. The commitment of generosity and justice to which our democracy calls us has, across the historical record, tended to dissipate the farther one stands from the dominant center of English-speaking, white, male prosperity. Recent immigrants limited in English proficiency, females, people of color, and low-income families have consistently experienced *less* access to opportunity. This is so widely acknowledged and so long-standing that many in a position to do something about it fail to act, as if concluding that if something could have been done about it, it would have been done already. After all, the poor will always be with us.

As educators in a democracy, we bear a special responsibility to do what we can, within the realm of where our influence can be felt, to ensure that the children under our care, all of them, do indeed enjoy equal access to the life opportunities for which we serve as the gatekeepers. More than citizens at large, it is our job to serve *in loco parentis* as advocates for all children. We must break our own embedded tendency—whether rooted in culture or psychology or human genetics—to favor certain groups and individuals (those who look like us, act like us, speak like us) at the expense of others.

107

To generate some historical insight into the ongoing failure of our society and our educational institutions to act with generosity and justice, we examine this chapter's "case in point." But this time, we proceed differently. We will explore not just one case, but several. In significant ways, each of the schools showcased in previous chapters faced the opportunity to act on the twin imperatives of generosity and justice. Therefore, we will briefly examine each one. How did each one respond to the opportunities that its particular moment and setting provided? Are these schools examplars of right conduct? The record is mixed. Although each of these five schools managed to swim against the cultural tide in admirable ways, as we have seen, perhaps one area in which they, as a group, stumbled was the call to attend to all children within their realms of influence.

Case in Point

We begin with the Beaver Country Day School because its response represents the sort of good intentions, sound pedagogy, and unfortunate shortsightedness that characterizes much in the history of otherwise thoughtful school practice. Where its pedagogy was firmly progressive, its vision of social justice was decidedly not. Many of us who have advocated vigorously for progressive school practices while attending less to issues of social justice will, if we are honest, recognize some aspect of ourselves in the early stance of the school's leaders. Though they proudly trumpeted their alliance with progressive education principles, they clearly did not ally themselves with a progressive social agenda. Tuition, though not as high as other private schools of the day, was nonetheless set well beyond the reach of the middle and lower classes, at $450 a year for the lower school and $500 for the upper school.[1] The founding families represented Boston's liberal upper crust. A *Boston Evening Transcript* article appearing at the founding of the school leads with "Prominent Boston men and women have interested themselves in this new school. . . ."[2] A *Cambridge Tribune* article from the same period discusses the location of the school in the "delightful section of the aristocratic Brookline district of greater Boston."[3] It mentions also that the Educational Advisory Board had originally been chaired by Charles W. Eliot, president of Harvard University, and included other luminaries from Harvard, Bryn Mawr, and Johns Hopkins.

Insight into the politics of the Beaver School community is revealed in a straw poll conducted by student editors of the school's literary magazine for the 1936 presidential election. Results showed 139 votes for Republican challenger Alf Landon and 45 for incumbent Franklin D. Roosevelt. Student opinions, of course, are not necessarily representative of parent opinions, except that, in this case, the editor reporting these results notes, "Very few of us have made up our minds for ourselves. What our families believe we believe. . . . What we hear at the dinner table we accept as our gospel, unquestioned."[4] As a centrist within the Republican Party, Landon was the Republicans' best chance against a strong incumbent, FDR. Landon lost with just 37 percent of the popular vote, eight electoral votes, and carried only Maine and Vermont.[5] In the midst of FDR's sweeping progressive social reforms, Beaver's "progressives" were clearly not on board.

The school's blindness to social justice is apparent in its faculty's assessment of opportunities for service by students to the greater community. In a historical essay by Beaver faculty, the authors lament, "The school finds itself handicapped in respect to providing actual participation in out-of-school community life. It is located in one of the most completely serviced towns in the United States. . . . Consequently . . . it cannot find much that is genuine in the line of actual service to a community."[6] Had the faculty been paying attention to the devastating effects of the Great Depression on families and neighborhoods three miles down the road in Boston proper, they surely would have found service opportunities galore!

Perhaps most telling is the transcript of a session held in 1946 by a Boston University professor with members of the Beaver community. The following exchange speaks volumes:

[Prof. Mahoney]: "Democracy is the kind of society in which free men strive to the end that all may share equitably."

Miss Clendinin: "Private schools have a difficult problem. How can we justify the denial of intermingling?"

Ans.: Don't worry too much. It is a justifiable fact of liberty.

After a few further remarks, the meeting was adjourned.[7]

Like the Beaver Country Day School that was spawned by it, the Progressive Education Association (PEA) displayed a commitment to progressive pedagogy without a concomitant commitment to a progressive social agenda. Among the thirty schools in the famous study of which Beaver was a part, no school served predominantly black or lower-class students. Though the organization as a whole was heedless of race- and class-based discrimination, within the PEA there was at least one very prominent voice asserting a strong progressive social agenda. George Counts delivered a speech at the annual meeting of the PEA in 1932 that was later widely pamphleted. In his *Dare the Schools Build a New Social Order?* he attacks the self-satisfaction of the liberal elite, whom he viewed as the substance of the progressive movement,

who, in spite of all their good qualities, have no deep and abiding
loyalties, possess no convictions for which they would sacrifice
over-much, would find it hard to live without their customary
material comforts, are rather insensitive to the accepted forms of
social injustice, are content to play the role of interested spectator
in the drama of human history.[8]

Beaver's costly private school tuition, its singularly white, upper-middle-
class constituency, and its apparently Republican leanings place it squarely in
the crosshairs of Counts's sharp analysis. At the same time, it should be noted
that the Beaver Country Day School provided an elite education to girls at a
time when the best schools were for boys. It sent a generation of women into
the world with the confidence, knowledge of the system, and critical skills to
assume leadership roles and help lay the foundation for a feminist movement
a generation later.

In our own times, much has changed at the Beaver Country Day School.
As of this writing, the school is headed by Peter Hutton, who is in the process
of bringing the school back to its original pedagogical principles and, in contrast
to the school's founders, is seeking to bring greater diversity to the student
body and faculty. The school has made significant gains on both fronts, with
some 26 percent of students receiving financial aid, 26 percent of the student
body comprised of persons of color, and 20 percent of the faculty comprised
of persons of color.[9]

We turn next to Bronson Alcott's Temple School. Though its demise was
sealed with Alcott's intemperate public statements, a post–1837 epilogue shows a
stunning act of courage by Alcott. After being forced to close the original school
on Tremont Street, Alcott reopened the school at his home four months later
with fifteen pupils. In June 1839, he admitted an African American girl pupil.
He must have known the risk he was taking. Shortly, the parents of Alcott's
white pupils demanded that the black child be dismissed. Alcott's journal entry
reads: "Decline dismissing the child and, June 22nd, have five children remaining
as pupils—my own, W. Russell's, and Robinson's."[10] Perhaps more scandalous
than "obscene" classroom talk, Alcott dared to racially integrate his school.

Nonetheless, Alcott's record on matters of social justice remains mixed.
The Temple School was not a public school. Parents paid a hefty tuition.
Alcott's journal entry of February 18, 1837, refers to a quarterly rate of $15.
In comparison, quarterly tuition at his earlier elementary school in 1828 was
just $7, and the per pupil expenditure for the Boston city schools in 1841
stood at $12.43 for the entire year.[11] The school's opulent conditions contrast
sharply with most schools of the time. It easily outstrips the dank and leaning
rural schoolhouses in Massachusetts but also the Boston primary schools, about
which one contemporary observer wrote:

We often found the entrance to the room through the filthy back-yard of a house, or in the neighborhood of a stable, or a blacksmith's shop, or a carriage manufactory house, where the children could scarcely pass in safety. . . . Several rooms are in the second or third stories, with steep and narrow stair cases, entirely unsafe for children.[12]

Alcott's Temple School represented a stark contrast to the schooling available to white children of Boston and an opportunity wholly unavailable to children of color.

The records of the Bethlehem Lab School and the Parker Charter School are also mixed. Both schools deny privileged access through the use of a lottery to determine admission. There is no test or interview to select students. However, because they are schools-of-choice, potential enrollees must be aware of their existence and the potentially advantageous opportunities that may be garnered from the progressive education they offer. The Bethlehem Lab School, by virtue of its location within a predominantly white, middle-class community, draws from an already privileged population. The Parker School, on the other hand, draws from forty communities—suburban, rural, and urban—that surround it. One need not be able to afford the high cost of real estate in a privileged community to attend the Parker School, unlike so many well-resourced suburban high schools. On the other hand, with no school bus service available, students must be able to get themselves to school on their own from miles away—a requirement that favors two-parent households of means. In addition, the lottery system, according to statute, does not set quotas for household income or ethnicity/race. Minority students who are admitted through the lottery face the daunting prospect of being possibly the only person of color in their class. Both the Lab School and the Parker School do not track students. All students have access to the same mix of classmates and equal access to high-quality curriculum and instruction.

Among the five schools profiled in this book, the one that reached most effectively across the divide of privilege—including class, ethnicity, and language—is the Quincy Public School system, under Francis Parker. The community of Quincy, Massachusetts, was, at the time of Parker's superintendency, populated largely by immigrant groups from Europe who were drawn to Quincy by employment opportunities in the granite industry. According to H. Hobart Holly's *Quincy, 350 Years*, the first-wave immigrants at mid-century were Irish. Italian immigrants began to arrive around 1860.[13] Both Irish and Italian immigrants were the target of nativist attacks throughout the nineteenth century. Were we to apply contemporary terminology to characterize the Quincy community of the day, it would include a large free and reduced lunch population with, no doubt, a high percentage of English language learners and recent immigrants. For such students to gain access to the power of thoughtful curricular and instructional practices is especially striking, given the kinds of scripted approaches so prevalent in contemporary urban settings.

Larger Lessons

Perhaps more than the other cultural conspirators that we have explored, the failure of generosity and justice feels like a problem beyond the purview of any single educator. None of us can change 400 years of culturally embedded attitudes. Consequently, we conclude that, yes, privilege is a problem, and we must establish progressive social policies, *at some policy level higher than our own*, to combat it. But we often fail to see the ways that we, in our daily actions, may combat it. We fail to see that just like all of the other culturally embedded tendencies we have examined, the fundamental elements of the system at work in such a large way *out there* are present in our daily lives, operating in just the same ways, but on a smaller scale.

Classroom Encounter

You wish more students would participate in class discussions, but the same five or six students carry the ball every day. The others—usually about twenty students—are mostly quiet. They're not bad. They don't make trouble—well, not much. But they don't add anything to the class. If you've ever felt this lament welling up inside you at the end of a frustrating day of teaching, then you are perfectly normal. A minority of students seems to do most of the work and would appear to be learning the most. You certainly are not discriminating in your behavior as a teacher. You call for volunteers to answer questions, and you will happily call on anyone who raises a hand, but only a few—the same few every day—take you up. You are ready to provide extra help after school, but mainly just those students who are always volunteering in class and generally doing well anyway come occasionally to your after-school sessions. You read everyone's papers, and you offer the same balance of critical comments embedded in positive, encouraging language. You try to show an interest in everyone. You are a decent, caring teacher who tries hard. What more could you do?

The problem is not in the quantity of work you do, since you already spend hours outside of school preparing lessons and reading student work. The problem is that you rely on voluntarism to drive student engagement. Those who volunteer to engage will learn. Those who decline the invitation will not. The irony is that those who are volunteering tend to be the least in need of what you have to offer. The quiet and/or disengaged students making up most of the class are the ones who stand to learn the most but who end up learning the least. It is in this way that schools, as a result of our daily practices, support the existing patterns of attainment and privilege as opposed to serving as agents for social change. Jean Anyon, in a classic piece of scholarship conducted nearly thirty years ago, demonstrated how the social and economic class of a child's home tends to predict the sort of experience a student will have in school and serves to prepare the student for occupying the same social and economic class as his or her parents. In her study, Anyon simply sat in the back of the room of schools serving communities that were predominantly one social/economic stratum (working class, middle class, and professional/elite). She found that the quality of instruction and the nature of classroom interactions generally closely mirrored the relationship of adult workers to their work for each class. Students in the school serving the working-class community who experience the humdrum of worksheets in a chaotic and rule-bound setting were being prepared for "future wage labor that is mechanical and routine."[14] Students in the school serving the affluent, professional community experienced an inquiry-driven, project-based curriculum that developed "skills of linguistic, artistic, and scientific expression."[15] Does our invitation-only approach to classroom engagement reinforce the patterns of behavior that are embedded in the social and economic backgrounds of the students who enter our classroom? Whether or not it does—and there is reason to believe it does—we will do well to take a more assertive stance toward student engagement by employing teaching strategies that both *invite and compel* student participation. Any good text on inclusive teaching methods will offer excellent suggestions. For example, "Think-pair-share" is an effective way to open up class discussion to wide participation. Students are sometimes reluctant to speak up in class discussion because they are frightened by the prospect of working out their ideas out loud in front of a full class. All of us, at some time or other, have probably felt this way as a youth or as an adult. If, however, students are given the opportunity to work out their thinking quietly and then to construct a response with just one other person, they will be more willing to share their thinking with the whole class. Think-pair-share is a simple technique that grants students an intimate audience of one classmate with whom to practice constructing a response to a teacher prompt before sharing ideas with the whole class. First, the teacher offers the prompt to the whole class, giving students time to *think* quietly about their response to the prompt. Next, the teacher asks students to *pair* with one another to hear each other's response. Finally, the teacher calls on individual students to *share* their responses with the whole class. This simple technique increases classwide engagement in learning and can dramatically increase active participation in class discussions.[16] By employing strategies such as these, we create a classroom climate that not only invites students to participate but equips them with the resources they need to do so effectively and then pushes them to move just beyond their comfort zone.

As we attempt to counter the culture of class-based privilege, we need also to attend to privilege that is rooted in culture and language. Michaela Colombo, a scholar and practitioner in the field of cultural and linguistic diversity, urges mainstream teachers, approximately 90 percent of whom are white, to develop "cultural competence," which she defines as "the ability to understand diverse perspectives and appropriately interact with members of other cultures in a variety of situations."[17] Colombo says that we need to immerse ourselves in diverse cultures so that we can experience the sense of isolation and disequilibrium that diverse learners experience daily in mainstream American classrooms. This builds empathy, but, she adds, we must go farther and gain understanding of the diverse cultures of the students with whom we interact. Colombo urges teachers of culturally and linguistically diverse learners to "get to know families in their homes, neighborhoods, or places of worship. Talk with parents and discover the diverse strengths within families. Explore family customs and history and make these an integral part of your curriculum.[18] Colombo offers a useful reading list that can help any teacher get started with this work. Her list appears in the Notes section of this chapter.[19]

Teacher Talk

The dynamics of privilege and invitation-only instruction play themselves out in the school as a whole very similarly to the way they play out in the classroom. Anyon's observations from thirty years ago hew closely to the varied experiences of students in tracked classes in many comprehensive high schools today. Privilege finds its way to the honors and AP classes where the tone and pedagogy are most like the "professional elite" classrooms. Students with less social capital tend to populate the "general" track and often experience instruction like that of the "working-class" school.

As much as these disturbing patterns have been documented by Anyon, Jonathan Kozol, Jeannie Oakes, and others,[20] they nonetheless persist. It is as though we understand and acknowledge the problem in general, but in our own school, we deny its existence. Perhaps it is time we treated some of our practices in schools the same way therapists treat addiction—with interventions based on confrontation. Instructional practice in the classroom is the heart and soul of our work, yet, as Richard Elmore has persuasively demonstrated, instructional practice is an aspect of schools that organizationally we fail to really pay attention to.[21] In fact, Elmore shows, the system has evolved in a way that insulates instructional practice from public exposure and external intervention.

There is a movement under way to change that. The advent of professional learning communities and related work that focuses on collaborative examination of instructional practice and student assessment by colleagues working together in the same school is perhaps the most promising innovation in contemporary education.[22] Its power lies in the focus it takes on instructional practice, not in the abstract but in the specific. If one of the great problems of public education is the widely inconsistent quality of instruction that students experience both between and within schools, then the surest way to begin to address it is to break through the layers of insulation and denial that have protected it. Interestingly, the one school among the five schools featured in this book that most successfully broke through culturally embedded privilege was the one that focused most heavily on instructional practice. Superintendent Parker was an instructional leader long before the term was coined. Teaching practice was public and openly examined in a collegial, supportive, and system-wide push to improve the quality of learning for all students. The results, examined in chapter 1, suggest that his effort extended the benefits of high-quality instruction to a community that more commonly experienced what Anyon described for the working-class school 100 years after Francis Parker.

Public Engagement

"Parents tell me they are concerned that the quality of the AP classes will suffer if they are opened up to just anyone. And I hear the teachers aren't too happy about it either." The president of the school board, with whom you enjoy a good rapport, is sitting across from you in the café where you have met for lunch. As superintendent of schools, you have been exploring ways to increase access for more students to the highest-quality instruction and highest-status curriculum available. You have been discussing with your staff and the board the possibility of removing the requirement for a teacher recommendation in order to enroll in the history and English AP classes and opening them up to any student who wishes to enroll and is willing to participate in a summer prep program, for which you have obtained funding. You chew your food and listen. Your board president continues, "The junior and senior years, in particular, are when students need to demonstrate achievement. If anyone can take the AP classes, then they become meaningless as a mark of distinction. And, from an educational standpoint, it waters down what the teacher can do because the teacher has to teach to the middle."

In this classic, cordial face-off between you and your board president, equity is positioned as the enemy of excellence. Grant all students access to the best, and the best will be reduced. Grant all students access to the best, and you lose your ability to mark some as better than others. The social attainment system, based on selectivity, requires that some *not* be selected. Mess with that dynamic and you mess with a cherished cultural myth. The failure of generosity and justice persists, because it is cloaked in the more palatable cultural belief in meritocracy. Work hard and you will succeed. Strive and you will rise to the top.

What is needed is a fundamental shift in attitude both among educators and among the public at large. We need to shift away from a definition of success that is norm referenced and replace it with meaningful expectations for student learning that are criterion referenced. We need to shift away from a system of high grades and selective courses for the few and instead strive to educate all students to high standards of knowledge and understanding. The mechanisms by which this is achieved—opening up the AP courses, detracking departments, busing students across districts, equalizing per pupil expenditures—are simultaneously crucial and secondary to the *shift in belief* that is needed to drive them. A cultural consensus must be forged from the twin ideas of equity and excellence, not as enemies of one another but as necessary ingredients for democracy and social harmony. As social reformers, we fail sometimes because we push for the mechanical changes without engaging those who disagree with us in a deeper conversation about justice, democracy, and social harmony. The work of psychologist Rob Evans, described in chapter 1, is instructive here. If we expect people to change, Evans advises, then we need to convince them that maintaining the status quo is riskier than attempting change. If we can succeed first in establishing a consensus around the need for change, then the conversation about the mechanics of change will be much readier to move forward constructively.

Beginning that conversation can be daunting. As with other challenging conversations, sometimes it is best to begin with data collection. Ask your staff the following questions:

1. Who are the students best served by our school district? What are the experiences they have in school that serve them well?

2. Who are the students least well served by our school district? What are their experiences in school? What can be done to make the experiences of the second group more like the experiences of the first group?[23]

These questions advance no agenda other than the noncontroversial goal of serving all students equally well. However, an honest exploration of the answers to these questions can be a first step into deeply transformative work. Subsequently, a presentation of the findings to the board of education could begin the process of discomforting the public with the status quo and clearing a path in the direction of change.

Another strategy, with a somewhat sharper edge, is to ask, within the scope of your own practice, who gains from the decision I am making? Who loses? If it were my child, would this be an acceptable loss? There is nothing like personalizing the impact of a decision to gain clarity around the question of its fairness.

Countering the Culture

Several themes emerge from the cases and from our exploration of strategies for countering the culture. They follow:

1. Move beyond invitation-only instructional practices. Engaging all students requires deliberate pedagogical moves by us. It is not enough to invite participation. It must be structured to gently but insistently include all students.

2. Open up instructional practice for professional dialogue. If we hope to move beyond invitation-only instruction and change our practice to focus on inclusivity, then we need collegial support. Breaking through the insulation that surrounds instruction is a difficult and crucial first step. Fortunately, this is increasingly recognized in the field, and there are organizations and strategies ready to support the work.

3. Engage in the deeper conversations about the risks of the status quo and the relative safety of change. Instrumental discussions about how to achieve greater equity that take place without an exploration of the reasons change is necessary will almost inevitably crash on the rocks of sabotage, subterfuge, and blame. Engaging in the deeper conversation will loosen the soil and increase the chances that instrumental discussion, to be held at a later stage, will go more smoothly.

4. Develop the habit of asking, who gains from this decision? Who loses? If it were my child, would this be an acceptable loss?

Case Closed

When it comes to our sixth conspirator, the failure of generosity and justice, the record of the five schools featured in this book is mixed. Efforts were sporadic, generally not strategic. Sometimes a blind eye was knowingly turned toward potential opportunities to counter the prevailing culture. How similar is our own record? Is it mixed? Are our efforts sporadic, generally not strategic? In what ways do we knowingly turn a blind eye toward opportunities to counter the prevailing culture? While some circumstances always lie beyond our direct control or direct influence, there are usually some that are under our direct control or within our arc of significant influence. It is there that we can choose to focus our attention, and it is there where we can accomplish our best work.

7

The Mindful Practitioner

As far as our public schools are concerned, we have become a nation of mindless adoption. Our problems are defined in terms of test scores and demographics; our solutions are off-the-shelf programs that promise results. Implementation is quick and on the cheap. We treat our teachers like an army of technicians who need only to be trained in a one-day workshop. And the half-life of most reforms is approximately equal to the tenure of the superintendent of schools. Meanwhile, the teaching force continues to work in isolation with little time for curriculum planning and student assessment, let alone collaborative reflection on instructional practice or student work. All of this mindless activity is reinforced by deeply embedded patterns of thinking: schools are like factories, fear impulsively drives our actions, planning is suited to the psychological needs of the planners, promising innovation is crushed by the gears of the system, goals proliferate, keeping us from doing anything well, and privileged groups gain at the expense of everyone else. All in all, it sounds pretty hopeless.

However, none of this is inevitable. We can change the system. The system we have is the consequence of deliberate actions taken by powerful groups at key moments in the history of education, those who pushed back against the system that was. "The way it is" is not the way it has always been, nor must it always be. *We can change the system.* The system we have is the consequence of people who changed their system in an earlier day. They did so by seeing over the high walls of the systems that bounded the vision of most people of their day. We can do likewise, but to do so we must first recognize that the system is *us,* which means we must change ourselves. Systemic change begins with personal transformation. As we transform our own habits of thinking, we begin to change our practice. As our practice is transformed, it presses up against the norms of the system. If enough of us exert enough pressure against established routines, structures, and policies, then a compelling argument for change is made in action. Large-scale change becomes possible. It all begins with mindful practice.

Mindful practice, for an educator, requires a deep awareness of the culturally embedded habits that work against thoughtful schooling, a deliberate commitment to personal transformation of one's own habits, and an active, strategic agenda for change within the system, three simple, powerful moves:

1. Deep awareness. We must first and foremost gain an awareness of the contingent nature of our circumstances. Our circumstances are neither permanent nor unchangeable. They exist because of forces that are temporarily joined into a state of equilibrium. Historical knowledge, offered through three of the case studies in this book, is one way to build awareness. History shows us both the powerful cultural traits that manifest themselves across time as well as the form-shifting nature of human institutions as they respond to groups and individuals bent on social change. Study of contemporary social change, featured in two of the case studies in this book, is another way to see over the high walls of the dominant system and to catch a glimpse of other possibilities. There are other ways to see beyond the system as it is: anthropology, systems analysis, organizational psychology, economics, political science. All represent ways of knowing that allow us to transcend the world as most people experience it. They constitute a ladder that we may climb to the top to gain a full and liberating awareness of our surroundings.

2. Personal transformation. The second requisite step is to recognize that to the extent that we have become socialized within a particular system, we incorporate its essential elements into our own psyches and literally become the system that surrounds us. Take a group of people out of their culture, relocate them to a desert island, and pretty soon—assuming they survive—they will replicate in inventive ways and with local materials, the artifacts of their home culture, because the patterns of thinking of their culture reside deeply inside each of them. Only with a deep awareness that allows us to experience other possibilities, other ways of thinking and acting, can we begin to change ourselves, and then only through deliberate and insistently regular reflection on our daily practice. Old habits die hard. We must labor to adopt new habits.

3. A strategic agenda for systemic change. Once we begin to transform the system that is inside us, we create a disequilibrium between our own thought and actions and the patterns of thought and action demanded by the system. That state of disequilibrium may be resolved in either of two ways: either we relent and resubmit to the old habits of mind on which the system is based, or we force an opening in the system with enough space for us to practice different ways of thinking and behaving. Educators in the five schools featured in this book did just that, all with at least some success. Each did it through the adoption of a strategic agenda for change that was idiosyncratically responsive to their particular cultural surround.

Deep awareness, personal transformation, and a strategic agenda for change can lead to significant outcomes, as the five schools featured in this book bear testimony. The result of such work, however, is not simply to erase one's culture. That is neither desirable nor possible. Rather, the successful outcome is an inventive adaptation of existing cultural resources to achieve more constructive ends. This process we will call mindful adaptation. Deep awareness, coupled with personal transformation and a strategic agenda for change, is the process of mindful adaptation. Mindful adaptation is the antidote for the dominant practice of mindless adoption.

With this in mind, let's review the major arguments and suggestions from each of the chapters. Understanding the culturally embedded tendencies against thoughtful schooling—our six cultural conspirators—grants us deep awareness. Observing the examples of the five schools that broke through and countered the dominant culture helps us understand the means of personal transformation and the power of a strategic agenda for change. And observing the contours of school practice in each of the five schools demonstrates the varied possibilities of mindful adaptation across time and place. What follows is a quick review of where we've been and what we've learned, organized according to the six conspirators against thoughtful schooling.

The Manufacturing Metaphor

The manufacturing metaphor is the tendency to think about schools in the way we think about factories that manufacture products. There are inputs (programs) and outputs (tests), raw material (children), and products (knowledge affixed to children). The danger, of course, is that such thinking results in educational practices that are well suited to inert raw materials and highly inappropriate to children. In contemporary schooling, the language and mindset of industrial manufacturing are deployed with particular harm in urban schools serving poor and minority families. Jonathan Kozol has dramatically documented related practices in *Shame of the Nation*. Our chief example of a school that broke through the language and mind-set of manufacturing comes from over 100 years ago but is striking in its contemporary feel. Francis Parker, as superintendent of schools in Quincy, Massachusetts, was surrounded by the language and thinking of manufacturing. His community stood in the thick of an industrial revolution that defined schoolwork for the emerging industrial nation. Nonetheless, Parker framed his work and the work of his teachers in different terms, terms more appropriate to the growth and learning of children. His schools were admired across the country for their humanity and efficacy and for their thoughtful educational practices.

In our own talk and our own actions, we need to demonstrate our commitment to thoughtful educational practices. We need to avoid manufacturing language and adopt language that better represents the complexity of learning and respect for students and adults engaged in it. Reframing our thoughts and language in environmental/ecological terms brings us into a more harmonious relationship with the way in which children actually learn and grow. Also, initiating work that is framed by an environmental/ecological view will force those with whom we engage to adopt the same frame, in this way provoking a similar transformation in others.

The Fear Factor

The fear factor is the tendency of fear to drive school activity. The danger is that fear promotes impulse, not deliberation. School activity driven by fear is inevitably impulsive and reactive. The power of fear to drive school policy and practice is readily apparent across the historical record, where American public schooling has been driven by fear of oppressed groups, fear of perceived enemies beyond our borders, and fear of global economic competition. Nearly 200 years ago, educator Bronson Alcott launched a school characterized by a belief in the essential goodness of children, in direct opposition to the old Calvinist fear of Satan. But the community grew afraid of an educator who was crossing boundaries of social propriety. Driven by fear, the community turned against Alcott and his school. Alcott, ignoring the power of community fear, failed to save his fragile enterprise. Fear can grip a nation, or the community served by a single school, or the school staff, or its leader. Fear arises from the perception of loss of control. Since change inevitably involves the loss of control, then fear is the regular companion of any school reformer. Engaging those at the receiving end of school change in questions that get at the need for change and supporting them with resources to make change possible will help restore a sense of control and overcome fear through the very process of change. Providing both challenge and support in this way assists reformers in steering between the Scylla and Charybdis of the comfort of the status quo and the fear of overly ambitious innovation.

The Grand Interlock

The grand interlock is the tendency of the system to crush promising innovation. Conversely, it is also the tendency of the system to judge the acceptability of an innovation not by its value to student learning but by its fit among the gears of the larger system. The local history of many school districts is littered with promising innovations that disappeared not because they failed to serve students well but because they were worn down by the gears of the system in which they were situated. In this chapter, our example of an innovation that broke through the cultural barriers is the Bethlehem Lab School. Through a careful initiation process, the school was able to open up sufficient space within the system to introduce a significant enhancement of student learning, even though it did not easily fit among the spinning gears of the existing system. The story of this school suggests that successful innovation requires a dual focus on the content of the innovation and the political and cultural context into which it is being introduced. Because the innovation runs to design standards that are different from the system that surrounds it, a workable interface must be crafted. As with an organ transplanted into a new host, the possibility of rejection is strongest at the beginning—it tapers somewhat with time, but it never really disappears. Continuous monitoring and adjustment of medication are crucial!

The View from the Top

The view from the top is the tendency to make plans and decisions that are psychologically satisfying to the planners and decision makers rather than judging the appropriateness of plans and decisions based on the impact at the ground level of student learning and instructional practice. The current national infatuation with curriculum frameworks generated by federal and state departments of education, as well as professional education associations, is a prime example. Frameworks are judged by the degree to which they cover all of the content for which all of the competing voices of the polis clamor. The consequence at the ground level of student learning and instructional practice is curricular overload and student alienation. The Francis W. Parker Charter School serves as an example of a school that has managed to counter the view from the top with curriculm design based on a principle that, in learning, "less is more," and that student engagement is best achieved not by a tidily crowded agenda but by provocative questions, hands-on projects, and performance-based assessment. Reformers who strive to counter the view from the top need to ask their relevant communities, what learning is most important? What are the "enduring understandings" and capacities that we want our students to walk away with? How can we most effectively engage our students in learning? In short, we need to come down from the policy and planning mountaintop to observe the needs and the means to serve those needs at the ground level of the classroom.

The Politics of Appeasement

The politics of appeasement is the tendency to say yes to all legitimate requests. The danger is that in trying to be all things to all people, we end up doing nothing well. We observe the politics of appeasement all around us in the accumulation of goals, programs, and expectations through legislative mandates layered onto schools from above and our own impulse to please the varied publics we directly serve. The story of the Beaver Country Day School demonstrates both the power of sticking with a clear, defining mission and the danger of attempting to please constituents at the cost of institutional purpose. Reformers who seek to counter the politics of appeasement will do well to hold a steady focus on a school's mission and to judge the appropriateness of new programs, new initiatives, and new directions by their relevance to the school's central purpose.

The Failure of Generosity and Justice

The failure of generosity and justice is the tendency to favor certain groups at the expense of others. We see this tendency in the contemporary world of schooling in the uneven allocation of resources among neighboring and equally "public" school districts. We see it also in our own practice every time we favor a child without considering the cost to his or her classmates. In this chapter we observe that for all five schools featured in this book, the record is mixed on their commitment to serving all students equitably. The Beaver Country Day School and the Temple School excluded students who could not afford tuition. The Parker School and the Bethlehem Lab School exclude students who are not lucky enough to live in homes where the parents are knowledgeable about school options and familiar enough with the system to know how to exercise those options. However, we have also seen that Francis Parker brought a boldly progressive education to low-income, immigrant families. We have observed that Bronson Alcott crossed the color line generations ahead of his time. We have also seen the Beaver Country Day School train its focus deliberately on the enrollment of students of color and on the hiring of faculty of color. And we have seen that enrollment to the Bethlehem Lab School and the Parker School is governed by a socially leveling lottery. Reformers who seek a greater commitment to the ideals of generosity and justice must examine their own practices and ask themselves the following questions: In what ways do I favor certain groups and individuals? Who wins and who loses from my decisions? If it were my child, would I find this an acceptable loss?

Prevailing against the Dominant Culture of Schools

Each of the schools profiled in this book offers a unique approach to countering the cultural conspiracy that works against thoughtful schooling. Each school appeared in a particular time and place and was formed by individuals who had a distinct vision of good schooling. Nonetheless, there is a common trait that pulses through all five schools—each is characterized by a persistent habit of inquiry and reflection, and each was founded by people who asked probing questions about the nature of childhood, the meaning of education, and the purpose of schools. The inclination to ask such questions played a role not only in establishing the school but in marking the institution as a place characterized by the regular asking of questions. Inquiry and reflection became the modus operandi of each one. Inquiry and reflection are, at the deepest level, each school's essential curriculum.

This book has posited a conspiracy theory. Specifically, it has argued that there are deeply embedded cultural traits that conspire against thoughtful school practice. Nonetheless, some schools—such as the five in this book—counter the culture and break through. Anthropologists tell us that you cannot escape your culture. You can never really leave it behind. Culture is destiny. How is it, then, that some schools achieve fundamental change? Is it possible that the conspiracy theory offered in this book represents only a partial view of American educational culture? Is it possible that even while there are elements of our national culture that conspire against thoughtful schooling, there are, perhaps, other elements of our national culture that are the wellspring of reflective practice and innovation? There must be, because thoughtful schools do not just appear *sui generis*!

Culture may, in some respects, be likened to a genetic code. In the same way that DNA determines physical traits, culture determines our essential patterns of thought and behavior. And just as in genetics there are dominant and recessive physical traits, so too in culture we may construe certain patterns of thinking and behavior as dominant and others as recessive. In this book we have identified the dominant traits as "conspirators." But what other traits, possibly recessive, reside in our cultural gene code that allow for the emergence of thoughtful schools and thoughtful practice? The answer could well be the subject of another book, but several immediately suggest themselves: innovation, optimism, pragmatism, teamwork, fairness, charity, justice, democracy, responsibility, reciprocity. These, too, are deeply embedded in American culture. And these are the cultural resources, the cultural tools, that reformers may draw upon—have drawn upon—in establishing and sustaining thoughtful school practice

Our goal is nothing short of cultural transformation, a daunting mountain of a job. It is easy to become overwhelmed, to lose hope, to drift into despair. When I find myself overcome by the work to be done, I am reminded of a passage from Jewish tradition, "Do not be daunted by the world's grief. Do justly, now. Love mercy, now. Walk humbly, now. You are not obligated to complete the work, but neither are you free to abandon it."[1] I don't need to make it all the way up the mountain, but if I can help some number of us make it part of the way, then I have met my responsibility to contribute to the good of the world.

What the Talmud expresses so beautifully in spiritual and moral terms, psychology helps us understand in pragmatic terms with the notion of locus of control. Popularized by Julian Rotter in an article first published in 1966,[2] locus of control theory suggests that different people tend to link events in their lives causally to forces that are either internal (i.e., under their own control) or external (i.e., beyond their own control). Life, of course, presents us with both kinds of events. Wisdom lies in rightly understanding which events are under our influence and which are not. Perhaps it is even more helpful to understand locus of control as a scale. At one end are those events that are under our direct control. At the other end are events that we have no influence over whatsoever. In between, where most events occur, we have degrees of influence. The admonition that we ought to carry with us into our work as reformers is to focus on what we can do within our realm of influence, within our locus of control. Don't focus on what lies beyond your realm of influence (outside your locus of control), because that will lead to feelings of defeat and ultimately to a loss of effectiveness as an educator. No matter what your circumstances, no matter how restrictive, you can always choose to focus on those events within your locus of control. Long-term prison survivors, whether they are Holocaust survivors, POWs, or Gulag-confined dissidents, regularly tell of the rituals and activities in which they engaged to maintain their sense of control, dignity, and, ultimately, their sanity under extreme conditions. They survived because they focused on what they could do, despite their inhumanly restricted realm of being. If you are a teacher, then you may have only limited influence on state policy, but you have very direct influence on the lives of the children you teach. As a superintendent of schools, you may rail against the contractual constraints against reform, but you can still exert strong influence over instructional practice among your teachers. For situations that call on you to counter the cultural conspirators against thoughtful schooling, consider the following questions as a guide to conserving your personal energy, deploying your personal resources constructively, and holding that overwhelmed feeling of despair at bay! Ask yourself the following, and then act accordingly: (1) What is the problem I wish to solve? (2) What roles do I play relative to the problem (e.g., educator, parent, grandparent, public official, state resident, U.S. citizen, etc.)? (3) How influential am I in each of the roles I play (controlling influence, significant influence, minor influence, no influence)? What can I do from the standpoint of each role? (4) What actions can I take right now in the medium term (this year into next year), and in the long term (two years plus)?

In focusing on your locus of control, it is important to remember that you play more than one role in the societal drama. Perhaps you are a teacher and within that role you have some influence over what happens in your classroom but not over the curriculum that you are handed. Nonetheless, you are also a resident of a community that has some sort of board of education that holds open meetings at which policy is discussed, where you have a right to public input; you are a resident of a state and have a state-level representative to the state legislature; and you are a U.S. citizen and have a representative and two senators in Washington, D.C. You also can join advocacy groups, as Frequent opportunities arise for public input into the development of policies within the state departments of education. You play multiple roles, and for each role there is an avenue along which you can make constructive noise! By rationally understanding where the power of our influence lies, and by deploying our talents and energy accordingly, we can avoid despair and walk in the company of efficacy and hope.

Notes

Introduction: A Conspiracy Theory

1. Larry Cuban, "Managing the Dilemmas of High School Reform," *Curriculum Inquiry* 1 (2000): 105–118.

Chapter 1: The Manufacturing Metaphor

1. Jonathan Kozol, *The Shame of the Nation: The Restoration of Apartheid Schooling in America* (New York: Crown, 2005). (Note: For a window into the ways in which business thinking dominates contemporary schooling, see especially Chapter 4, "Preparing Minds for Markets.")

2. David Tyack and Larry Cuban, *Tinkering toward Utopia: A Century of Public School Reform* (Cambridge, MA: Harvard University Press, 1996).

3. *New England Journal of Education* 92, vol. 36, no. 5 (December 29, 1892): 411–412. This is a memoir written by a teacher who taught in Quincy all through the 1870s, including the Parker era. He recalls, contrary to contemporary popular accounts, that it was Smith, not C. F. Adams, who began the direct examination of pupils by school committee members.

4. "Report of the School Committee," *Annual Report of the Town of Quincy, Massachusetts,* 1873, 6–7.

5. "The New Education in the Public Schools of Quincy, Mass. (1879), from Charles F. Adams, *The New Departure in the Common Schools of Quincy* (Boston, 1879), 33–40, in *Education in the United States: A Documentary History,* vol. 3, ed. Sol Cohen (New York: Random House, 1974), 1811.

6. Ibid.

7. Allen Johnson, ed., *Dictionary of American Biography*, vol. 1 (New York: Scribners, 1957), 50.

8. See Jack K. Campbell, *Colonel Parker: The Children's Crusader* (New York: Teachers College Press, 1967), esp. 77–78.

9. "Report of the Superintendent," in "Report of the School Committee," in *Annual Report of the Town of Quincy, Massachusetts,* 1876, 120.

10. Annual Report of the Town of Quincy, Massachusetts, 1874, 11, and Annual Report of the Town of Quincy, Massachusetts, 1876, 14.

11. See note 5 above.

12. Annual Report of the Town of Quincy, Massachusetts, 1876, 118.

13. Annual Report of the Town of Quincy, Massachusetts, 1888, 15 (Schools Addendum).

14. Annual Report of the Town of Quincy, Massachusetts, 1881, 200.

15. *New England Journal of Education*, vol. X, no. 16, 265 (no date appears).

16. *New England Journal of Education*, vol. XXI, no. 3 (February 1, 1883), 71.

17. *New England Journal of Education*, vol. XXI, no. 3 (February 1, 1883), 71.

18. Anna Brackett, untitled article in *New England Journal of Education*, vol. XI, no. 7 (February 12, 1880).

19. *New England Journal of Education*, vol. X, no. 12 (October 9, 1879), 197.

20. *The Quincy Patriot*, April 21, 1900, p. 1.

21. Teacher Departures from the Quincy Schools

Year	Teachers Departing or Moving Internally	Source
1876	13	Annual Report AR, p. 144
1878	16	AR, p. 155
1880	18	AR, p. 200

22. *The Quincy Patriot* notes Parker's resignation as "Post Commander" for the Grand Army of the Republic in Quincy upon Parker's departure as superintendent in 1880 (*The Quincy Patriot*, May 22, 1880, p. 2).

23. Citations in the *New England Journal of Education* are based on the *New England Journal of Education* semi-annual index for the period 1878–1892).

Year	C. F. Adams	F. W. Parker	Quincy	Total
1878	0	0	0	0
1879	0	1	5	6
1880	1	1	7	9
1881	0	0	1	1
1882	0	1	0	1
1883	0	0	1	1
1884	0	0	0	0
1885	0	2	0	2
1886	0	1	0	1
1887	0	1	0	1
1888	0	3	0	3
1889	0	0	0	0
1890	0	0	1	1
1891	0	2	1	3
1892	0	0	1	1
Total	1	12	17	30

24. Visitation of the Quincy Schools

Year	Number Reported	Source
1877	2,199	Annual Report (AR), p. 141
1878	3,196	AR, p. 177
1879	6,396	AR, p. 189
1880	10,714	AR, p. 199
1881	13,276	AR, p. 231
1882	10,008	AR, p. 213
1883	7867	AR, p. 243
1884	6,023	AR, p. 181
1885	5,271	AR, p. 57
1886	5,961	AR, p. 45
1887	7,549	AR, p. 41
1888	9,517	AR, p. 38

25. Robert Evans, *The Human Side of School Change: Reform, Resistance, and the Real-Life Problems of Innovation* (San Francisco: Jossey-Bass, 1996).

26. Ibid., 55.

27. Richard J. Murnane, Presentation for "Redesigning the American High School," Summer Institute sponsored by Harvard Graduate School of Education, Cambridge, MA, August 1, 2005. See also, Richard J. Murnane and Frank Levy, *Teaching the New Basic Skills:Principles for Educating Children to Thrive in a Changing Economy* (New York: The Free Press, 1996).

28. Ibid.

29. George Lakoff and Mark Johnson, *Metaphors We Live By,* 2d ed. (Chicago: University of Chicago Press, 2003), 3. See also George Lakoff, Howard Dean, and Don Hazen, *Don't Think of An Elephant:Know Your Values and Frame the Debate—The Essential Guide for Progressives* (Chelsea Green, VT: Chelsea Green Publishing Company, 2004).

30. Annual Report of the Town of Quincy, Massachusetts, 1884, 155.

31. Annual Report of the Town of Quincy, Massachusetts, 1881, 191.

Chapter 2: The Fear Factor

1. Cited in John D. Pulliam and James J. Van Patten, *History of Education in America,* 7th ed. (Upper Saddle River, NJ: Merrill, 1991), 51.

2. Earl Morse Wilbur, *A History of Unitarianism,* vol. 3 (Boston, MA: Beacon Press, 1945), 433.

3. Charles Beecher, ed., *Autobiography, Correspondence, etc., of Lyman Beecher, D.D.* 2 vols. (New York: Harper and Brothers, Publishers, 1871), vol. 2, 110, cited in Stanley K. Schultz, *The Culture Factory: Boston Public Schools, 1789–1860* (New York: Oxford University Press, 1973), 61.

4. Robert H. Lord, John E. Sexton, and Edward T. Harrington, *History of the Archdiocese of Boston in the Various Stages of Its Development, 1604 to 1943*, vol. 2 (New York: Sheed and Ward, 1944) 126, 179–204.

5. Stanley K. Schultz, *The Culture Factory: Boston Public Schools, 1789–1860* (New York: Oxford University Press, 1973), 50.

6. Horace Mann, *Value and Necessity of Education*, 4. Cited in Schultz, 54.

7. Cited in Odell Shepard, *Pedlar's Progress: The Life of Bronson Alcott* (New York: Greenwood Press, 1968 [original ed., 1937, Little, Brown, and Company]), 97.

8. Ibid., 120–121.

9. A. Bronson Alcott, *Record of Mr. Alcott's School Exemplifying the Principles and Methods of Moral Culture*, 3rd ed., rev. (Boston, MA: Roberts Brothers, 1874 [First ed., 1836; true author appears to be Elizabeth Palmer Peabody, who refers to herself in the preface to the original edition as "recorder."]).

10. Ibid., 14–15.

11. Ibid., 42.

12. Ibid., 29.

13. Ibid., 14.

14. Ibid., 20.

15. Ibid., 25–26.

16. Ibid., 30–31.

17. Ibid., 35.

18. Shepard, *Pedlar's Progress*, 173.

19. Ibid., 204.

20. Ibid., 186.

21. Ibid., 189.

22. Ibid., 193.

23. Ibid., 193–194.

24. Odell Shepard, ed., *The Journals of Bronson Alcott*, vol. 1 (Port Washington, NY: Kennikat Press, 1966). Journal entry for "April Week XV" of 1837, p. 88.

25. Richard L. Herrnstadt, ed., *The Letters of A. Bronson Alcott* (Ames: Iowa State University Press, 1969), 31.

26. Cited in Shepard, *Pedlar's Progress*, 204.

27. Herrnstadt, *The Letters*, 33.

28. Shepard, *Pedlar's Progress*, 204.

29. Attributed to Margaret Mead on a park bench plaque, University of Massachusetts, Lowell, South Campus, Main Quad. Original source not found.

30. Alcott, *Record*, 255–256.

31. Peter Marris, *Loss and Change* (New York: Anchor Books, 1975), 166. Cited by Michael Fullan, *The New Meaning of Educational Change*, 4th ed. (New York: Teachers College Press, 2007), 22.

32. Margaret Geanisis, personal e-mail communication, June 4, 2008. You may visit Ms. Geanisis's Web site at www.artistcolony.com.

33. Fullan, *The New Meaning of Educational Change*, 22.

34. Michael Baldassarre, principal of Gardner High School in Gardner, Massachusetts (at press time, director of Student Support Services in the Ralph C. Mahar Regional School District in Orange, Massachusetts).

Chapter 3: The View from the Top

1. Several sections in this chapter are adapted from material I wrote previously in a book about the Parker School. Reprinted by permission of the publisher. From James Nehring, *Upstart Startup: Creating and Sustaining a Public Charter School* (New York: Teachers College Press, Columbia University, 2002).

2. Robert B. Downs, *Friedrich Froebel* (Boston: Twayne Publishers, 1978). See also Michael Steven Shapiro, *Child's Garden: The Kindergarten Movement from Froebel to Dewey* (University Park: Pennsylvania State University Press, 1983).

3. Jack K. Campbell, *Colonel Parker: The Children's Crusader* (New York: Teachers College Press, 1967).

4. W. Aiken, *The Story of the Eight-Year Study with Conclusions and Recommendations* (New York: Harper and Brothers, 1942).

5. Theodore R. Sizer, *Horace's Compromise: The Dilemma of the American High School* (Boston, MA: Houghton-Mifflin, 1984).

6. Chester E. Finn Jr., Bruno V. Manno, and Gregg Vanourek, *Charter Schools in Action* (Princeton, NJ: Princeton University Press, 2000).

7. Finn et al., *Charter Schools*, 23.

8. Sizer, *Horace's Compromise*, 214.

9. See the official Web site of the Coalition of Essential Schools at www.essentialschools.org.

10. See the Parker School's "Criteria for Excellence" for a complete list of skills representing the school's learning standards. Available at www.parker.org.

11. See, for example, Robert E. Slavin, *Cooperative Learning: Theory, Research, and Practice* (Boston, MA: Allyn and Bacon, 1994).

12. Sizer, *Horace's Compromise*.

13. Arthur G. Powell, Eleanor Farrar, and David K. Cohen, *The Shopping Mall High School: Winners and Losers in the Educational Market Place* (Boston, MA: Houghton-Mifflin, 1985).

14. Denise Clark Pope, *"Doing School": How We Are Creating a Generation of Stressed Out, Materialistic, and Miseducated Students* (New Haven, CT: Yale University Press, 2001).

15. Go to www.cce.org (official Web site of the Center for Collaborative Education) for full information about the Boston Pilot Schools.

16. Jacqueline Ancess, *Beating the Odds: High Schools as Communities of Commitment* (New York: Teachers College Press, 2003).

17. Nehring, *Upstart Startup*. Also see James Nehring, *The School Within Us: The Creation of an Innovative Public School* (Albany: State University of New York Press, 1998).

Chapter 4: The Grand Interlock

1. A portion of this chapter is adapted from material I wrote previously in a book chapter about the Bethlehem Lab School. See "Teachers Leading Change: The Bethlehem

Lab School," in *Reflective Practice in Social Studies Education,* ed. E. Wayne Ross, (Bulletin No. 88, Washington, DC: National Council for the Social Studies, 1994).

2. Paulo Freire, *Pedagogy of the Oppressed* (New York: Continuum, 1986), 31.

3. Wilford M. Aiken, *Adventures in American Schooling, Volume I: The Story of the Eight-Year Study* (New York: Harper and Brothers, 1942).

4. Frederick L. Redefer, *The Eight-Year Study—Eight Years Later, A Study of Experimentation in the Thirty Schools.* Unpublished doctoral dissertation, Teachers College, Columbia University, dissertation approved February 5, 1952, 70.

5. Michael B. Katz, *Reconstructing American Education* (Cambridge, MA: Harvard University Press, 1987).

6. David Tyack and Larry Cuban, *Tinkering toward Utopia: A Century of Public School Reform* (Cambridge, MA: Harvard University Press, 1995), 57.

Chapter 5: The Politics of Appeasement

1. "Another Country Day School for Boston," *Boston Evening Transcript,* February 15, 1921.

2. See the 1923–1924 brochure for the Beaver Country Day School, BCDS Archives.

3. Transcript of speech given by Eugene Randolph Smith, April 1920, BCDS Archives.

4. Prospectus, Beaver Country Day School, 1923, p. 8, BCDS Archives.

5. Ibid.

6. Unlabeled flyer, Founding Records 1, Box 4, BCDS Archives.

7. "Professional Activities of the Beaver Country Day School, during the First Half Year, 1924–1925," BCDS Archives.

8. "A Rather Unique Educational Enterprise, Prospering Wonderfully," *Cambridge Tribune,* July 30, 1927.

9. *Adventures in American Schooling, Volume 5: Thirty Schools Tell Their Story* (New York: Harper and Brothers, 1943), 46.

10. Ibid.

11. See Dean Chamberlin, Enid Straw Chamberlin, Neal E. Drought, and William E. Scott, *Did They Succeed in College? The Follow-up Study of the Graduates of the Thirty Schools, Vol. IV,* in the series *Adventure in American Education* (New York: Harper Brothers, 1943).

12. *Time* magazine, December 24, 1945, p. 58.

13. Frederick L. Redefer, *The Eight-Year Study—Eight Years Later, A Study of Experimentation in the Thirty Schools.* Unpublished doctoral dissertation, Teachers College, Columbia University. Approved February 5, 1952.

14. Sawtell, Box no. 1, BCDS Archives.

15. "Finance Committee" (file), Folder 19, BCDS Archives.

16. Treasurer's Report, 1947, BCDS Archives.

17. Undated notes, c. 1946–1947, BCDS Archives.

18. Unlabeled flyer, Founding Records 1, Box 4, BCDS Archives.

19. See note 27 above.

20. Clearinghouse Committee Minutes, February 24, 1943, BCDS Archives.

21. Ibid.

22. Grant Wiggins and Jay McTighe, *Understanding by Design, expanded 2nd ed.* (Alexandria, VA: Association for Supervision and Curriculum Development, 2005).

23. Ibid., 71.

24. Roger Fisher and William L. Ury, *Getting to Yes: Negotiating Agreement without Giving In* (New York: Penguin, 1991).

25. Redefer, *The Eight-Year Study*, 70. Note: Though the author does not identify the school, characteristics identified in the text strongly suggest the school's identity.

26. "Beaver Country Day School," promotional brochure produced by Beaver Country Day School, Aline Gery, director of admission and financial aid, 2001.

27. Ibid.

Chapter 6: The Failure of Generosity and Justice

1. Brochure for the Beaver Country Day School, April 1921, BCDS Archives.

2. "Another Country Day School for Boston," *Boston Evening Transcript*, Tuesday, February 15, 1921, available in BCDS Archives.

3. "Professional Activities of the Beaver Country Day School, during the First Half Year, 1924–1925," BCDS Archives.

4. *The Beaver Log,* November 1936, BCDS Archives.

5. Current Biography (New York: H. W. Wilson and Company, 1944 [reissued 1971]), Alf Landon entry, 376–381.

6. *Adventures in American Schooling: Thirty Schools Tell Their Story* (New York: Harper and Brothers, 1943), 46.

7. Clearinghouse Committee Minutes, April 26, 1946, Sawtell, Box 1, BCDS Archives.

8. George Counts, *Dare the Schools Build a New Social Order?* (New York: Arno Press, 1969, 5–8; reprint of 1932 ed., published by John Day Company of New York).

9. See www.bcdschool.org., the official Web site of the Beaver Country Day School, accessed August 19, 2007.

10. Odell Shepard, ed., *The Journals of Bronson Alcott, Volume I* (Port Washington, NY: Kennikat Press, 1966), 210.

11. Shepard, *The Journals*, 88.

12. Report of the Primary School Committee on Improvements, Boston, 1833. Cited in Stanley K. Schultz, *The Culture Factory: Boston Public Schools, 1789–1860* (New York: Oxford University Press, 1973), 85.

13. H. Hobart Holly, *Quincy, 350 Years* (Quincy, MA: Quincy Historical Society, 1974).

14. Jean Anyon, "Social Class and the Hidden Curriculum of Work," *Journal of Education* 162:1: 67–92: 88.

15. Ibid.

16. Frank T. Lyman, "The Responsive Classroom Discussion: The Inclusion of All Students," in *Mainstreaming Digest*, ed. A. Anderson (College Park: University of Maryland Press, 1981), 109–113.

17. Michaela W. Colombo, "Empathy and Cultural Competence: Reflections from Teachers of Culturally Diverse Children," *Beyond the Journal, Young Children,* (November 2005): 2, accessed May 29, 2007, http://www.journal.naeyc.org/btj/200511/ColomboBTJ1105.pdf.

18. Ibid., 6.

19. Colombo's suggested reading list includes:

Delpit, Lisa. *Other People's Children: Cultural Conflict in the Classroom*, rev. ed. New York: New Press, 2006.

Nieto, Sonia. The Light in Their Eyes: Creating Multicultural Learning Communities. New York: Teachers College Press, 1999.

Paley, Vivian Gussin. *The Girl with the Brown Crayon*. Cambridge, MA: Harvard University Press, 1998.

Paley, Vivian Gussin. *Kwanzaa and Me: A Teacher's Story*. Cambridge, MA: Harvard University Press, 1996.

Paley, Vivian Gussin. *White Teacher, New Edition*. Cambridge, MA: Harvard University Press, 2000.

20. Jeannie Oakes, *Keeping Track: How Schools Structure Inequality* (New Haven, CT: Yale University Press, 1986); also see Jean Anyon, "Social Class and the Hidden Curriculum of Work," *Journal of Education* 162:1: 67–92: 88; Jonathan Kozol, *The Shame of the Nation: The Restoration of Apartheid Schooling in America* (New York: Crown, 2005).

21. Richard F. Elmore, *School Reform from the Inside Out: Policy, Practice, and Performance* (Cambridge, MA: Harvard Education Press, 2004).

22. See Richard Dufour and Robert E. Eaker, *Professional Learning Communities at Work: Best Practices for Enhancing Student Achievement* (Bloomington, IN: Solution Tree, 1998) See also www.nsrfharmony.org, the official Web site of the National School Reform Faculty.

23. These questions were developed by the author and colleagues Richard Elmore, Katherine Merseth, and Joseph Arangio for *Redesigning High Schools for Improved Instruction*, a program of the Harvard Graduate School of Education Programs in Professional Education.

Chapter 7: The Mindful Practitioner

1. Rabbi Tarfon from *The Mishnah* (Avot Tractate of the Order Nezikin).

2. Julian B. Rotter, "Generalized Expectancies for Internal versus External Control of Reinforcements," *Psychological Monographs* 80 (1966): 609.

Index